Zachary Taylor's Army
In Texas

From Corpus Christi to the Rio Grande. 1845-1846

Murphy Givens

Zachary Taylor's Army in Texas

From Corpus Christi to the Rio Grande. 1845-1846

Murphy Givens

Nueces Press

Corpus Christi, Texas

Library of Congress Control Number 2021919520
Zachary Taylor's Army in Texas
Author: Givens, Murphy

Includes bibliography.
    1. Mexican war
    2. Texas — History.
    3. Corpus Christi History
    4. South Texas History
    5. Zachary Taylor
    6. U. S. Grant
    7. United States Army

ISBN   978-1-7339524-4-6

Published by Nueces Press, Corpus Christi, Texas.

Cover design by Jeff Chilcoat

www.nuecespress.com

CONTENTS

PUBLISHER'S NOTE

Murphy Givens died on December 27, 2020 after a year-long battle with lung cancer. This is the last book he was able to write. Years ago, he had written *Zachary Taylor in Corpus Christi*, but was unsatisfied by the first book and wanted to delve deeper into the subject of Taylor and his army. He has included all the actions in Texas through the first two battles of the Mexican War, after which Taylor moved into Matamoras unopposed.

Givens used first-hand accounts of men who were in Texas with the army and early histories of the war to document the actions of the army. There were many West Point officers in command of the army. These well-educated men kept diaries, mailed letters to family and friends and wrote books on their experiences in the Mexican War and, later, the Civil War documenting their experiences.

Corpus Christi was unique in American history, with half of the U.S. Army encamped on one place. Taylor had six months to mold his troops into an organized fighting army. His successful efforts showed as the army defeated superior numbers of Mexican troops at both the Palo Alto and Resaca de la Palma battles.

Givens has woven the daily life in Corpus Christi and the long march south to the Rio Grande into a comprehensive history of the U. S. Army in South Texas preparing to defend the United states' claim to all of Texas to the Rio Grande.

Jim Moloney
Nueces Press

AUTHOR'S PREFACE

On a hot summer day, the steamer Alabama, after an easy run across the Gulf from New Orleans, anchored at sundown off St. Joseph's Island. Next morning the early risers of the 3rd Infantry Regiment lined the taffrail to get a glimpse of Texas. It was Saturday, July 26, 1845.

This was the summer Texas ratified annexation with the United States. Fearing trouble with Mexico, Gen. Zachary Taylor was ordered to move his command from Fort Jesup, La., to the disputed territory between the Nueces and Rio Grande. Taylor brought his army to Henry Kinney's trading post of Corpus Christi. Nearly 4,000 soldiers, half the total in the U.S. Army, were eventually in training on the outskirts of the village. Taylor changed his nomenclature from "Army of Observation" to "Army of Occupation."

From the first day of their arrival on Aug. 1, 1845, the soldiers put up tents and killed rattlesnakes in the high weeds along the shore. Defensive earthworks were thrown up, military order emerged, and Taylor called the encampment "Fort Marcy" after William Marcy, secretary of war.

The town south of the camp mushroomed, growing from about 100 in population to more than 2,000 people, a fair number of them saloon-keepers and camp followers.

In late November, a norther brought incessant rain and on Dec. 3 the temperature dropped to 23 degrees. Cold-stunned fish were gathered along the shoreline. Soldiers surrounded the camp with brush to screen the bitterly cold wind.

In February 1846, as Texas joined the Union, Taylor prepared to move to the border. On March 8, the first units marched out of town with the regimental band playing "The Girl I Left Behind Me." Within days, the tents were gone, nearly 4,000 soldiers were gone, and most of the town's 2,000 transient inhabitants departed to follow the army.

The regiments, spaced a day apart, marched down a route that was later called "Taylor's Trail." On March 20, the four brigades re-formed to cross the Arroyo Colorado, under threat of Mexican opposition, which failed to materialize. On March 28, the American flag was raised on the Rio Grande as the people of Matamoros watched from across the river.

Ground was broken for a fortified enclosure called "Fort Texas" and later renamed "Fort Brown."

On May 8, Taylor's small force, returning from the supply depot at Point Isabel, came in sight of Gen. Arista's army drawn up for battle at a place called Palo Alto, "high brush." The battle began and ended as an artillery duel. Some 320 Mexican soldiers were killed and nine Americans. Next day, the armies clashed again at an old riverbed called Resaca de la Palma. In the confused fighting that led to a rout, Arista lost nearly 2,000 men while 33 Americans were killed.

These were the first battles fought in the Mexican War. The victories made Zachary Taylor a national hero and helped propel him to the White House. The seven month stay at Corpus Christi determined the direction of later events and helped set the course of history. It is the story of a small army preparing for the war to come.

Capt. Daniel Whiting of the 7th Regiment reflected on what the army gained during its concentration at Corpus Christi. Whiting thought that it afforded the opportunity for "unlimited association" between officers and that, "All sectionality and jealousy of feeling was overcome . . . from which association may be dated that esprit de corps that afterwards prevailed throughout the war."

Oliver Otis Howard, a major general in the U.S. Army, wrote that while the army was at Corpus Christi it "became strong and conscious of its strength under the leader the soldiers believed in. This was an esprit de corps hard to produce but, when produced, hard for a foe to overcome."

Young officers who were at Corpus Christi in 1845-46 made history in the Mexican War and later in the Civil War. The most prominent was U.S. Grant. Robert E. Lee was not with Taylor at Corpus Christi, though he may have visited the encampment from San Antonio. He joined Taylor at Monterrey. Others who became famous generals in the Civil War included George Meade, Braxton Bragg, James Longstreet, John F. Reynolds, Lafayette McLaws, George H. Thomas, Abner Doubleday, William Hardee, John Magruder, E. Kirby Smith, Richard Gatlin, Alexander Hays, and Samuel G. French.

The letters, diaries and memoirs of these future generals make a great contribution to our understanding of the build-up to the Mexican War. I have drawn freely from these sources to compose a narrative of events stretching from Fort Jesup to Fort Brown to the first clash of arms. This was an important time, 175 years ago, with the drawing together of opposing forces leading to the inevitable collision at Palo Alto and Resaca de la Palma. It was arguably the most important time in the history of Corpus Christi, especially the early history of the town, and it is from that parochial perspective that I approached this work.

—Murphy Givens, June 2020

CHAPTER 1

Orders for Texas

It was now high summer of 1845, when the days were long and the nights were short. During the past year, in the presidential contest in 1844, the campaign slogan of James K. Polk of Tennessee was "All of Texas and all of Oregon." After Polk, the Democratic candidate, defeated Henry Clay of Kentucky, the Whig candidate, Col. Ethan Allen Hitchcock made a prescient note in his diary at Fort Jesup, La.[*] "We have certain intelligence that J. K. Polk is elected president. I look upon this as a step towards the annexation of Texas, first, then in due time the separation of the Union."

A step toward the annexation of Texas.
Yes, and very quickly. It happened even before Polk was inaugurated.

Annexation resolutions were introduced in Congress during the waning days of the John Tyler administration. They were passed, after a struggle, on March 1, 1845, with a slim majority in the House and Senate. They were quickly approved by President Tyler, who wanted to deny Polk the credit for adding another star to the Union. The Ninth Congress of the Republic of Texas soon followed suit.

---

[*] The fort was named for Brig. Gen. Thomas Sidney Jesup.

Mexico was quick to react. It warned that any attempt by the United States to annex Texas, which it considered a rebellious province, would lead to war. Juan Almonte, Mexico's foreign minister in Washington, demanded his passport and before his departure called the planned annexation "an act of aggression" that would despoil a friendly nation of her territory. Mexican diplomats in Paris and London notified the French and British governments that war was inevitable.

Mexico tried an end run by offering to recognize the Republic of Texas if it would reject annexation, but the gambit failed. The Republic of Texas and the United States held that Texas achieved its independence by hard fighting on the battlefield at San Jacinto, and was free to make up its own mind without interference or coercion from Mexico.

In the spring of 1845, the United States seemed eager for war. The "New Orleans Tropic" asked, "Who's for Mexico?" The "New York Morning News" asked — after the annexation of Texas was approved — "Who's the next customer, California or Canada?" The "Illinois State Register" said if war came over annexation then the United States should forcibly add Mexico to the Union.

Who's for Mexico? Who's the next customer?

Not all were itching for war. A sardonic editorial in the "New York Journal of Commerce" said, "The world has become stale and insipid, the ships ought to be all captured, and the cities battered down, and the world burned up, so that we can start again. There would be fun in that. Some interest, something to talk about."

People had a nebulous idea of what war would entail. The historian Bernard DeVoto wrote that war was "militia-muster day, it was volunteers shooting Seminoles in the Florida swamps, it was farmers blowing redcoats to hell from behind stone walls, most of all it was embattled frontiersmen slaughtering Wellington's veterans at New Orleans."

And more, "It was rhetoric, vague glory, and at bottom, something that did not imply bloodshed."

Some fun, some interest, something to talk about.

In London, "The Times" said, "When the United States government, with the full sanction of the American people, consummated the annexation of Texas, they should, according to all the usage of civilized governments, have proceeded to take military means for the protection of their new frontier." And that was what the James K. Polk administration proceeded to do: take military steps to protect the new frontier of Texas.

A MILITARY FORCE was being concentrated in western Louisiana at Fort Jesup on the Sabine River, south of Natchitoches, and at smaller installations of Camp Wilkins and Camp Salubrity nearby. Fort Jesup, said one officer, was nothing like a fort, "just a collection of huts and barracks."

At Camp Salubrity, a satellite camp near Fort Jesup, a young lieutenant named Ulysses S. Grant wrote that at first officers and men occupied ordinary tents but as the summer heat in Louisiana increased the tents were covered with sheds to break the rays of the sun. The hot summer was whiled away visiting other officers at Fort Jesup and socializing with cotton planters on the Red River and the citizens of Natchitoches and Grand Ecore.

There were exciting horse races at Natchitoches and, Grant wrote in memoirs, "I was there every day and bet low, generally lost. One of my comrades undertook to play "brag" at our camp and succeeded in ridding himself of twenty dollars, all in quarters. The game of brag* is kept up

---

* A card game similar to stud poker.

3

as lively as ever. I continued to play some and won considerable, but for some time back I have not played and probably will never play again — no resolution, though!"

Grant, after his games of brag, thought that the transfer of the 3rd and 4th regiments of infantry to western Louisiana was in no overt way linked to the prospective annexation of Texas. "Ostensibly, we were intended to discourage any filibustering into Texas, but really as a menace to Mexico in case she appeared to contemplate war." Grant found that generally the officers he knew were indifferent to the great political issue of annexation, but he was bitterly opposed and came to regard the resulting war "as one of the most unjust ever waged by a stronger against a weaker nation."

In that hot summer of annexation and talk of war, one question hanging over the legislative exercise of adding the Republic of Texas to the United States was whether the southern boundary of Texas was along the Nueces River — as Mexico claimed — or the Rio Grande 170 miles south.

For Texas officials it was the Rio Grande. They cited the existence of Henry Kinney's trading post at Corpus Christi, on the south side of the Nueces River at its mouth, as proof on the ground that Texas controlled the disputed region between the two rivers. In Washington, Secretary of State James Buchanan concurred that Kinney's outpost provided the legal justification for the U.S. claim that the southernmost boundary of Texas was the Rio Grande, not the Nueces, the River of Nuts.

At the time of the summer solstice on June 21, 1845, a month before Texas ratified annexation and seven months before the Republic would become a state of the United States, Gen. Zachary Taylor was ordered to move his little army from the pine woods of Louisiana to the coastal region of Texas. Taylor had been in command at Fort Jesup for a year, replacing Gen. Matthew Arbuckle as commander of the 1st Military District. Taylor was a veteran of the Black Hawk War in the Ohio Valley and the

Seminole wars in Florida and owned large cotton plantations in Kentucky and Louisiana.

By the end of the month, Secretary of War William L. Marcy in Washington sent Taylor orders directing him, when the annexation resolutions were accepted by Congress, to move his command to the western border of Texas. Marcy said the exact location was up to Taylor.

"Put your forces into position where they may most promptly and efficiently act in defense of Texas. Your ultimate destination is on or near the Rio Grande," said the War Department orders.

In additional instructions, Marcy stressed that Taylor should avoid overt acts of aggression and refrain from disturbing any Mexican posts on the left bank of the Rio Grande "unless an actual state of war should exist." In his reply to Marcy, Taylor said he understood and that "the department may rest assured that I will take no step to interrupt the friendly relations between the United States and Mexico."

Put your forces into position where they may most promptly and efficiently act in defense of Texas.

CAPT. W. W. S. BLISS (Gen. Taylor's chief of staff and soon to be his son-in-law; the Taylor family jokingly called him "Perfect" Bliss) read the orders to Ethan Allen Hitchcock. He commanded the 3rd Infantry, the Old Guard regiment that dated back to 1784. Hitchcock took note of the event in his diary:

> Bliss read the orders to me last evening hastily at tattoo. I have scarcely slept a wink, thinking of the needful preparations. There is much to be done. I am now noting at reveille by candlelight and waiting the signal for muster. Violence leads to violence, and if this movement of ours does not lead to bloodshed, I am much mistaken.

CHAPTER 2

Embarking at New Orleans

In the first week of July of 1845, the needful preparations moved forward on all levels as annexation rites proceeded toward consummation. In Corpus Christi, Henry Kinney wrote a series of letters to Maj. Andrew Jackson Donelson, the U.S. *charge d'affaires* in Austin, pointing out that the boundary should be the Rio Grande and not the Nueces River and that Corpus Christi would make an ideal location for the army when it moved to take up a position in Texas.

Andrew Donelson passed this on to Gen. Zachary Taylor, adding that the small trading post on Corpus Christi Bay was the most westerly point occupied by Texas and that "Corpus Christi is said to be as healthy as Pensacola."

Corpus Christi was in the disputed territory but not so far in as to provoke Mexico. As Kinney's letters to Donelson stressed, it was roughly the same distance of 170 miles to any potential trouble spot on the Rio Grande, from Laredo in the west or Matamoros in the south.

Put your forces into position where they may most promptly and efficiently act in defense of Texas.

TAYLOR PREPARED TO MOVE his army to carry out that instruction. Seven companies of the 2nd Dragoons (called "Drags" by other soldiers) would travel overland from Fort Jesup to San Antonio. The remainder of Taylor's regiments at Fort Jesup would be transported by riverboat to New Orleans and from there by steamship to the western coast of Texas at a still-to-be determined location. Orders were cut for other units around the country to join Taylor's command. Taylor had Corpus Christi in mind as the site for concentrating his growing forces, though he had no first-hand knowledge of the place or whether it was a suitable location for the army.

On July 7, the summer air in Louisiana was hot, damp and steamy as the 3rd Infantry under Lt. Col. Ethan Allen Hitchcock marched out of Fort Jesup. They camped that first night at Nine-Mile Spring, nine miles from Natchitoches, and next morning marched to the riverboat landing at Grand Ecore and embarked on two steamboats for New Orleans. The 4th Regiment under the command of Col. Josiah Vose preceded them to the Crescent City. Lt. Braxton Bragg of the 3rd Artillery arrived from Charleston to join his regiment.

The 3rd Infantry took up quarters at the Lower Cotton Press, adjacent to the Mississippi River, which cost the army $100 a day, a sum Hitchcock considered excessive.

Soon after their arrival in New Orleans, a soldier ran up and told Hitchcock that Col. Vose of the 4th, "a fine old gentleman," was dead. Hitchcock hurried to meet the surgeon who told him that Vose had been drilling his regiment and returned to his quarters where he fell and died. Hitchcock commanded the funeral escort next day, composed of men from the 3rd and 4th regiments.

Early one morning Lt. Ulysses S. Grant of the 4th Infantry Regiment found the early stillness of the streets shattered by a gunshot. Grant looked out his window and saw clusters of men and learned afterward it had been a duel, "a couple of gentlemen deciding a difference of opinion at twenty paces. I do not remember if either was killed, or even hurt, but no doubt the question of difference was settled satisfactorily. I do not believe I ever would have the courage to fight a duel."

On July 19, a day of melting heat, Lt. Braxton Bragg arrived from Charleston, S. C. with his company of the 3rd Artillery. Bragg was well-known in the army for his unyielding sense of honor and duty and, because of that his relationships with his superior officers were often strained.

At Bragg's last posting, at Fort Moultrie, he would not speak to his commanding officer, Col. Gates, except in an official capacity. The colonel, it was said, tried to repair the relationship as he came into the sutler's quarters at the post, which formed a sort of club. The colonel said to Bragg, "A glass of wine with you, sir!" Bragg, as unbending as he could be, said, "Col. William Gates, if you order me to drink a glass of wine with you, I shall have to do it."

The "Daily Picayune" suggested that the people of New Orleans would like to see a parade of at least two of the regiments but it was reported that because of the oppressive heat and the condition of the troops — 250 of whom were raw recruits — a general turnout was prevented.

Back at Fort Jesup, after the 3rd Infantry left for New Orleans, Gen. Taylor stayed behind to see the dragoons depart on their overland journey. The command consisted of seven companies of the dragoons, 450 men, with a large train of 60 supply wagons.

The dragoons took up a line of march under the command of Col. David Twiggs, a bull-necked, red-faced Georgian with white-fringed hair, great sideburns, and loaded with a rich vocabulary.

One historian described him as a human volcano "pouring forth a red-hot flood of orders from a crater of a mouth; he was vastly enjoyed by the rough soldiers even when he 'cursed them right out of their boots.' "

After the dragoons left Jesup Taylor traveled by the steamboat Yazoo to New Orleans. On board the river steamer, Gen. Taylor saw a fellow passenger who looked very familiar. It was Jefferson Davis, now in his mid-thirties.

A decade earlier, Lt. Jefferson Davis married Taylor's oldest daughter, Sarah Knox Taylor, against the General's express wishes. Taylor's daughter died soon after the wedding and there was a rift between the two men. On the riverboat steamer, Davis, a member of Congress from Mississippi, was bound for Natchez, where he was to take Miss Varina Howell as his second wife.

Despite old hard feelings between Taylor and Davis, "no trace of animosity marred the manner of either gentleman as the father-in-law met the son-in-law who had been a fellow sufferer in the greatest personal tragedy of both their lives," wrote historian Holman Hamilton. "Grasping Davis' hand, Taylor greeted him warmly and in the friendliest spirit wished him happiness in the new marital venture. Davis never forgot Zachary Taylor's change of heart."

On the trip down the river, Taylor shared a stateroom with a fellow traveler, a young man, who said the general "talked about planting and crops and the civil government of the country and appeared to be as ignorant of our army as if he had never seen it."

Taylor was 61 years old, a thickset man with stubby legs who, by all accounts, was more comfortable with farmers, planters and frontiersmen than gentlemen officers and indeed looked more like a farmer than a soldier.

The "Daily Picayune" reported on July 19 that the army chartered ships Queen Victoria and Suviah and the fast steam packet Alabama to transport the troops to Texas.

Advance units of Taylor's army embarked in the middle of the night on Tuesday, July 22, 1845. Lt. W. S. Henry wrote: "As we marched out, the moon was just rising, gilding the housetops, and caused our bayonets to glisten in the mellow light. The deep shadows on one side of the street, and bright moonlight upon the other, the solemn quiet of the sleeping city, disturbed so harshly by the martial music of the column, formed a scene which touched one's feelings, and will not easily be forgotten."

As Hitchcock's men of the 3rd Infantry marched through the streets of New Orleans, fife and drum of the regimental band played "The Girl I Left Behind Me":

> *I seek for one as fair and gay*
> *But find none to remind me*
> *How sweet the hours I passed away*
> *With the girl I left behind me.* *

They reached the waterfront an hour before midnight. The first aboard the transport ship Alabama were eight companies of the 3rd (567 men and officers); two companies were left behind in New Orleans. The Alabama left port at three a.m. on July 23 and passed a settlement of houses on stilts at the mouth of the Mississippi. The transport ship was escorted by a sloop-of-war, the USS St. Mary's, and Hitchcock noted in his diary that they were on their way "to plant the flag of the U.S. in Texas. Gen. Taylor is on board in command of the army of occupation." Part of the 4th regiment and 3rd artillery embarked on the Queen Victoria and other units of the 4th on the Suviah.

Three days later, on Friday, July 25, after "a delightful run" across the Gulf, the Alabama arrived at the Aransas Pass channel that divides the barrier islands of Mustang and St. Joseph's Islands, just across the bay from the small frontier settlement of Corpus Christi. The ship anchored off the southern end of St. Joseph's near the pass.

Early next morning, a fine summer day, the sky was turning light and the early risers lined the taffrail to get their first view of Texas. They realized the significance of the occasion and watched the shore with close attention. "It was the first glimpse of the promised land," wrote Lt. Henry, "the land of the lone star no longer."

---

* This old English folk song became popular with the American army in the war of 1812. Various versions of the song remained popular during the Mexican War, the Civil War and World War I.

CHAPTER 3

On St. Joseph's Island

Saturday, July 26, 1845: Col. Ethan Allen Hitchcock noted in his diary that they had arrived last evening within a few miles of the entrance into Aransas Bay and anchored for fear of running too far into the pass in the night.

"This morning, we came down to anchor off the entrance. We lay very still, all of us looking on shore and watching the motion of some two or three small sailboats beyond the island, one of which is supposed to be a pilot boat. After breakfast, some of us will go on shore in a small boat. Gen. Taylor seems anxious to get the men on shore on the island. Our lighters are not here and we do not know when they will be here."

That soon changed with the arrival of the small steamer Undine, which was hired by the army to convey troops and supplies as a lighter at $350 a day for 30 days.

With Taylor in a hurry to get the men ashore, Hitchcock sent Lt. Daniel Chandler to land to look for water. It was Saturday, July 28 at 9 a.m. Chandler put up a pole on one of the highest of the sand hills on St. Joseph's* and raised a small U. S. flag, the first American flag to fly over Texas

---

* The name of St. Joseph's Island was officially changed to San Jose Island on Jan. 10, 1973, by order of Judge John H. Miller of the 36th District Court based on a request by Perry Bass, who inherited the island from his uncle, independent oil magnate Sid Richardson.

soil. "It floats over a rich acquisition," said Lt. W. S. Henry, "the most precious Uncle Sam has yet added to his crown."

After the flag-raising, Lt. Chandler reported back to Hitchcock that it was almost impossible to find a readily available source of good drinking water. "But he landed near the western or southern extremity of the island," Hitchcock wrote, "and we saw that there were people living higher up the island, and we saw cattle besides. We sent a company off to land and then changed the position of the steamer, placing her nearly opposite the house and afterwards sent off two other companies."

Lt. Henry's company was the first to land and he found that the St. Joseph's beach and rolling sand hills "presented quite a bold and picturesque appearance, resembling the Florida coast. You miss, however, the palmetto and pine; to the latter-named we have bidden a long farewell. The live-oak, of immense size, through whose thickly-interlaced leaves and limbs the sun's rays never pierce, has taken their place."

Getting ashore was not easy. The Alabama, the fast steam packet that brought the 3rd from New Orleans, drew too much water to cross the bar. "It became necessary for us to land in small boats," wrote Henry. "Seventy-five yards distant from the shore the men had to jump overboard into the roaring surf. They made a frolic of it. Some old veteran camp women took to the element as if they were born in it while others, more delicately nerved, preferred a man's back to ride to shore."

They discovered that if they dug down four feet they would reach a table of fresh water. The resulting wells were lined with barrel staves to present the sandy sides from caving in.

"My company was encamped near a fresh-water pond," wrote Henry. "Within a few paces there was another pond of precisely similar appearance but salt as brine. I cannot account for the water in some places being fresh and in other's salt. The fresh water, at best, has a most unpleasant taste."

The last of the 3rd Infantry landed on July 28. Hitchcock found the tents of the regiment scattered up and down the island for three miles. St. Joseph's is about two miles wide and 25 miles long. At the southern end, near the pass, was Lt. Henry's K Company. Hitchcock had supper with Henry, who had supplied his company with fresh oysters, and returned for breakfast next morning for more oysters.

Companies G and E were three miles from the south end, facing the sea. Hitchcock thought they were tolerably well supplied with water. "We dig down the depth of a barrel and find water, but it is brackish. The eight companies of the 3rd Regiment have completed their landing with but little inconvenience."

The men found St. Joseph's delightful after the hot, soggy heat of Louisiana. They enjoyed the Gulf breeze and white-sand beaches and soldiers played in the surf like children. "The beach on St. Joseph's," wrote one lieutenant, "excels far-famed Rockaway for its bathing." Another wrote that, "There was nothing but the hot sun, but if you were in the shade, you are cooler than any place in the north."

Lt. Henry discovered that fishing off the island could not be beat; baited hooks were swallowed by drum, mullet, redfish, and many other varieties. The men caught great quantities of redfish, which were the most prized. Said Henry, "They bait with fiddlers, wade out into the surf, and as fast as they throw in their lines are sure to have a bite; not so sure, however, to catch the fish, for they often strike such large ones they snap their hooks like pipe stems. As soon as you have fastened one, you throw the line over your shoulder and pull for shore double quick."

MANY YEARS BEFORE, St. Joseph's had been the haunt of Jean Lafitte and his buccaneers. Lafitte's camp called

Campeachy on Galveston Island was burned in 1820 during a punitive raid by U.S. warships and Lafitte moved down the coast, taking refuge on St. Joseph's. His landing place was on the southwest end of the island.

When the pirate moved on, some of his men stayed behind and retired on St. Joseph's. Local legends said Lafitte's old pirates turned to new employment as "wreckers" — shining a light from the dunes to mislead a ship, cause a shipwreck and salvage the plunder. A lantern tied to a donkey's back going up and down the dunes looked from a distance like a ship bobbing at sea. A few years before, in the 1830s, a man was hanged on the island for "setting a false light."

The island was also home to a number of settlers, including a man named John Baker, Capt. Bludworth, William Roberts, an Englishman, Capt. Peter Johnson, a Dane, John Low, and James Mainlan. Most prominent of St. Joseph's settlers was James Babbitt Wells, who was a privateer during the Texas Revolution and commanded the Texas Navy yards at Galveston. Wells operated a cattle ranch on St. Joseph's; Lydia Ann Channel was named for his wife. These settlers were living on the island's northeastern end when the army arrived.

Hitchcock noted that he went to the house of the customs collector, George Collingsworth, and was surprised to find himself addressed by name by "an old sickly-looking woman" who said, "Mr. Hitchcock, don't you remember a family named Hastings in Virginia?" Hitchcock did not remember the family but the old woman said she was a daughter and was the widow of the late consul at Matamoros.

AS THE TROOPS DUG wells, set up camps, and cavorted on island beaches, Taylor had not decided where to concentrate the army and establish his headquarters. Henry Kinney's letters promoted Corpus Christi as the best site for the army encampment. Taylor had to weigh political as well as military considerations. As for the latter, there had been no advance reconnaissance to enlighten him.

Taylor took steps to remedy his lack of direct information. In a letter to Washington dated July 28, he wrote from the steamship Alabama that eight companies of the 3rd were camped on St. Joseph's and he was trying to decide whether to move to Corpus Christi or the area between where Rockport is today and Live Oak Point. "I am waiting for the report of a boat expedition sent to Corpus Christi Bay before I determine on the site of an encampment. The position will probably be Live Oak Point in Aransas Bay." He also asked the party to take a good look at McGloin's Bluff (where Ingleside is today).

Taylor next wrote the adjutant general that he was ready to establish the encampment at the mouth of the Nueces River "but the extreme shallowness of the water will, I fear, present an insuperable obstacle, unless we can procure lighters of much lighter draught than those we have at present." In his dispatch, Taylor wrote:

> The difficulties of effecting a debarkation on this coast and of establishing depots for supplying the army are much greater than I anticipated, and will render our operations at once embarrassing and expensive. Between Pass Cavallo and Brazos Santiago there is no entrance for vessels drawing more than seven or eight feet; and the prevailing winds render the operation of lightering extremely uncertain and hazardous.

Taylor finally made his decision that the site at the mouth of the Nueces River called Kinney's Rancho had certain advantages. There was a large flat tableland behind a high bluff where the troops could be drilled and Corpus Christi, as Taylor noted in a letter to Washington, "is healthy, easily supplied, and well-situated to hold in observance the course of the Rio Grande from Matamoros to Laredo, being 150 miles from several points on the river." Taylor was repeating Kinney's lobbying points of why Corpus Christi would be a good place to bring the army.

Corpus Christi was well-situated to hold in observance the course of the Rio Grande.

Though the village or rancho as it was called was in the disputed region between the Nueces and Rio Grande, claimed by Texas and Mexico, Taylor chose to accept the interpretation that it belonged to Texas by the right of occupation. And he was following the wishes of President Polk. A War Department telegram advised Taylor that, "The President desires at least part of your troops west of the Nueces." That was clear enough.

There were major disadvantages Taylor would soon discover. One was a shortage of fresh water, another was a lack of trees for fuel for cooking and campfires, and the most difficult was the shallow bay clogged with mudflats that would make it challenging to land men and supplies.

The challenge soon became apparent. The army's hired shallow-draft lighter Undine drew four feet of water. The depth of water over the extensive mudflats of the bay was three feet and a half, on a good day.

Hitchcock, always ready to advise Taylor, suggested the general keep the army on St. Joseph's until a strong southwest wind increased the depth of water over the shoals. But Taylor was in no mood to be instructed by a subordinate and ignored the tendered advice. He wanted to get the men settled at a place of encampment to prepare a defensive position for any aggressive moves Mexico might make.

CHAPTER 4

Landing on North Beach

Gen. Zachary Taylor ordered companies K and G of Col. Hitchcock's 3rd to sail across the bay on the Undine and set up camp at Corpus Christi. As Hitchcock had warned would happen, the vessel ran aground in the mudflats. On the morning of July 29 he wrote:

> Gen. Taylor is determined to take two companies on board the Undine and attempt to steam up the bay, though the Undine drew several inches over four feet and four feet was the deepest water that had been reported over the flats. This movement was made upon a hasty suggestion of Capt. (G. H.) Crosman, the assistant quartermaster, who saw the tide low when he first came on shore the evening of the 28th, and saw it a few inches higher on the morning of the next day. The general changed his mind two or three times about the movement, but two companies went on board the Undine and running up about five miles ran aground where there was only three and a half feet of water. She was then three or four miles from the flats. We remained aground all day and the following night.

As they lay aground, Hitchcock makes clear that he and the general did not see eye to eye on this. They were very different men. Hitchcock, a West Pointer, the grandson of

Revolutionary War hero Ethan Allen, privately in the pages of his diary showed that he had little respect for Taylor, who dressed like a farmer and cared little for army traditions.

Hitchcock was one of Taylor's foremost critics. He thought Taylor based his judgments on instinct and that he was more suited to physical than intellectual pursuits. His nickname, bestowed on him by newspapers from his days as an Indian fighter, was "Old Rough and Ready."

Critics said everything about Taylor suggested the coarse backwoodsman. One historian noted, "In speech he was rough and ungrammatical, in dress unkempt and even dirty, and in every external of his profession unmilitary. He never had seen a real battle or even a real army. West Pointers, trim in person and in mind, but inferior to him in strength, practical sense, and familiarity with men and things, he felt strongly inclined to belittle."

Taylor didn't look like the commander of an army. He dressed for comfort and rarely wore a uniform. He was fond of sitting slouched side-saddle on his horse. He was not the heroic picture of a military commander on a battlefield.

Taylor's manner and garb led to all kinds of stories about him and some of them were probably true, wrote Edward J. Nichols ("Zach Taylor's Little Army"):

> In one of them, a new lieutenant appearing to pay his respects saw an old man behind headquarters cleaning the general's — it must be the general's — sword. "A dollar to clean mine too?" he asked. "Sure thing." The old man turned out to be Old Zach. In another story two young officers in search of their general ran across a shabby old farmer. "How's crops, old fellow?" "Oh," he answered, "purty good." Before moving on, one officer said, "Give our love to the old lady." That

evening they caught up with the shabby old farmer in his headquarters tent.

"Gen. Taylor," said Capt. T. B. Kinder of Indiana, "looks more like an old farmer going to market with eggs to sell than anything I can think of; jovial and good-natured."

This "jovial old farmer" was easygoing and lax with the men. Justin Smith wrote that a burly private, a new recruit from Europe, failed to obey an order and Taylor grabbed him by the ears and began to shake him, a form of punishment called "wooling" in the army. Not accustomed to this kind of treatment, "the private was astonished, red-faced and angry, and knocked Taylor flat on the ground. As officers rushed up to grab the man, Taylor made them back off. 'Let him alone. He'll make a good soldier.' "

Hitchcock by contrast was a West Point martinet, a scholar who played a flute and studied mystical philosophy in his tent. He read Marcus Aurelius and Spinoza's "Ethics" (between severe bouts of diarrhea) and began a correspondence with Henry Wadsworth Longfellow "about the writings of the mystics whom Rossetti had translated."

Hitchcock had hundreds of books, which he liked to arrange and rearrange and organize. Unlike Taylor in almost every respect, he was an intellectual, a West Point professional, a stickler for military detail and for going by the book. The "Niles National Register" described him as "a complete scholar, a perfect gentleman, and a soldier."

Zachary Taylor was esteemed by many of the younger officers but not by Hitchcock. On an earlier tour of duty, when Hitchcock served as Taylor's adjutant, he lent Taylor a book — Hume's "History of England" — which Hitchcock dryly noted was probably the only book Taylor had ever read. "If he succeeds," Hitchcock said of Taylor at Corpus Christi, "it will be by accident."

Other, more junior officers, portray him in a better light. Lt. George Gordon Meade thought Taylor "a plain and sensible old gentleman." Lt. Ulysses S. Grant admired him and later wrote that he "was not an officer to trouble the administration much with his demands" but would make do with what he had. "Gen. Taylor never made any great show or parade, either of uniform* or retinue. In dress he was possibly too plain, rarely wearing anything in the field to indicate his rank or even that he was an officer. But he was known by every soldier in his army, and respected by all."

In an assessment of Taylor's ability by the "Niles National Register," the influential newspaper said "with his excellent good sense, there is no deficit in his character." That view was echoed by Lt. W. S. Henry of the 3rd Infantry, who wrote that Taylor was "a man of sound views and common sense (a pretty rare article these days)."

AS THE UNDINE LAY aground in the middle of the mudflats of the bay, Hitchcock fumed over Taylor's orders for the heavy load of provisions that had contributed to their plight.

"The general directed the assistant quartermaster to put on board 50 barrels," Hitchcock wrote. "Lt. Henry put on board an assortment of all parts of rations for the command for two weeks, but contained in 39 barrels. He asked me if that would not answer and I told him I thought so, but on his speaking to the general he was directed to add another 11 barrels of pork, the heaviest sort of freight, and this when he ought to have known it was impossible to cross the mudflats."

---

* Like Taylor, Grant preferred to wear civilian clothes instead of his uniform. When Grant first donned his uniform in 1843, as a second lieutenant in the 4th Infantry Regiment, he rode down the streets of Cincinnati, showing off, when a ragged urchin boy taunted him: "Soldier, will you work? No sir-ee! I'll sell my shirt first." The incident gave Grant a distaste for military dandyism that he never lost. (Memoirs)

If he succeeds, it will be by accident.

To lighten the load on the Undine, the men were put to work unloading freight until the boat was floated off and moved up to the shore of the mainland three or four miles away. Meanwhile, Taylor sent the captain of the steamer to examine the mudflats in person. He reported the depth of water over the flats was two feet and 11 inches.

Hitchcock said the general ordered everything out of the vessel, "the captain assuring him he could bring her down to three feet and six inches, and it was hoped she might be forced through the mud and then returning it was supposed a sort of channel might be made. The unloading proceeded until night set in.

Brick and bits of iron scattered about the boat were carried on shore, as well as all the baggage of the men, and this brought the boat down to the mark of three feet and seven inches. Still, the general and captain and quartermaster saw no reason for abandoning the original hope of forcing the boat over the flats."

Early on July 31, the Undine was put under steam and went over to within a few yards of the flats and there ran hard aground again.

"The captain (named Brice) was sent on the flats with a small boat but returned and reported what he ought to have known perfectly the day before," wrote Hitchcock.

"The mudflats could not be crossed. We dropped back a few miles to where the freight lay on shore (near today's Ingleside). By this time, several small fishing boats gathered around us and the general directed the quartermaster to hire them and ordered the two companies to board them. He was quite beside himself from anxiety, fatigue, and passion."

On one of the fishing boats was a man named Louis P. Cooke, a man with a past. He was a resident of Corpus Christi who had once been the second secretary of the

23

Texas Navy. Hitchcock and his adjutant boarded the small boat to make the 12-mile run across Corpus Christi Bay.

The men from the two companies transferred from the grounded Undine to the smaller vessels bobbing like corks in a peevish sea. They anchored 400 yards from shore and began to land on North Beach, generally known as Rincon then. Hitchcock noted in his diary:

> I am now here with two companies of the 3rd Infantry, companies K & G, probably the first troops to occupy the soil of Texas.*
>
> Corpus Christi is a very small rancho at the head of the bay of the same name. The citizens (several of them, a reception committee) have called to express their gratification at our arrival and offer assistance and information.
>
> All accounts agree that our safe arrival is little short of a miracle and is attributable to the mere accident of the bay being tolerably calm, for the people here say that on any ordinary day the wind would have raised such a sea as to have swamped some of the boats.

After K and G landed on July 31st, other companies of the regiment began arriving from St. Joseph's. "The regiment is gradually coming over the bay," Hitchcock wrote on Aug. 5. "E company arrived yesterday and last night the sloop Picayune brought my own baggage and part of the band."

One of Hitchcock's officers, Capt. Henry Bainbridge, was slow in landing his company and sent a note that he would land the next day since he wanted to sleep. Hitchcock sent him a direct order that brought him and his company ashore without delay. Hitchcock thought

---

* Hitchcock forgets that St. Joseph's was part of the "soil of Texas."

Bainbridge was too fond of his comforts.

"We hear that the 4th Regiment of Infantry is off the entrance into Aransas Bay and, further, that the steamer Monmouth has arrived, which Gen. Taylor ordered to be purchased in New Orleans as a lighter," Hitchcock wrote. "We have now two steamers in service, one hired and one owned, and neither can cross the mudflats."

If he succeeds, it will be by accident.

Taylor called the growing encampment at Corpus Christi Fort Marcy in an effort to flatter the Secretary of War, William Marcy, Taylor's superior. Most references to Fort Marcy are in Taylor's own dispatches. Whether it was a "fort" or not, they were camped, said one officer, on a pretty spot on the edge of the bay with weather so mild "it would rival France."

"Fort Marcy" was a camp of tents with improvised dirt embankments that Hitchcock had thrown up as a line of defense. The field work on the army's right, facing the bay, consisted of a sand-and-shell wall six feet high and 300 yards long. Not knowing what to expect, and since no artillery had yet arrived, Hitchcock borrowed two old cannons from Kinney, the founder of Corpus Christi. The cannon, Henry reckoned, "were more dangerous to ourselves than to any enemy."

The point taken by Taylor, said the "Niles National Register," was one of "extreme beauty, and one of the healthiest and pleasantest spots in world." The army was well-provisioned, said the Register, with wild deer, game of every kind, beef at two cents a pound (large, fat beeves were slaughtered daily for the troops) and the waters of Corpus Christi Bay "abound with fish and oysters."

Some of the senior officers brought with them servant-cooks who were adept at using what was available locally for their officer's mess.

Lt. Samuel G. French wrote of his commanding officer's exceptional cook:

> Maj. (Samuel) Ringgold carried with him a middle-aged colored servant who had much experience in arranging dinner parties in Baltimore. He cared for nothing save to surprise us with dishes that would have delighted Lucullus. Such pompano, baked red snappers, boiled redfish, delicate soups, turkeys, geese, ducks, and game birds on toast. In pastry he had no superior. Never could we, by money or otherwise, discover how he prepared his sauces. In taste in arranging a table he was fitted for a chef at Delmonico's or the Waldorf. With such a chef, every meal was a feast.

A letter printed in the "New Orleans Daily Picayune" said, "The army is now ready for action. It is well-appointed in every respect and every man able to do his duty and every heart a tower of strength. They are prepared and eager for a fray."

Regiments continued to arrive through August, September and October. Seven of the 10 companies of the 2nd Dragoons marched overland from Jesup and reached San Patricio on the Nueces River, 27 miles upstream from Corpus Christi, on Aug. 23. Three of the companies were left in San Antonio. In late August, the 7th Regiment of Infantry arrived, followed by the 4th Regiment in the first week of September, the 5th and the 8th in October.

By October, Taylor received his full complement of troops that were ordered to join his command, which included five regiments of infantry, one of dragoons, and four batteries of horse artillery. A duty roster showed 4,000 men — roughly half the entire U.S. Army at the time.

CHAPTER 5

A Mexican Hamlet

Before it was called Kinney's Rancho or Corpus Christi, the location along the curve of a great bay was known as the old Indian trading grounds, a place where traders landed contraband goods, like leaf tobacco, to avoid paying customs duties to the government of Mexico. They landed bales of cargo on the beach, loaded them on pack mules, and carried the smuggled goods into Mexico. This was the place later called Kinney's Rancho then the frontier settlement of Corpus Christi, where Zachary Taylor's troops landed on late afternoon of July 31, 1845.

Sixteen years before, in 1829, a trader named John J. Linn, landed tobacco at the old Indian trading grounds, with plans to haul his shipment to Camargo in Mexico. Linn found no settlement at the place that became Corpus Christi. Henry A. Gilpin, another trader, landed that same year with goods for sale in Mexico.

Surveyors camped on the site by the bay in 1838. "We saw no indication of any former settlement at this place," wrote Z. N. Morrell, "but were informed by an Irishman accompanying the surveyors that this was the point at which the colony of San Patricio" landed its supplies.

In September 1839, Henry Kinney, a 25-year-old merchant from Pennsylvania via Illinois, moved his trading operation from Live Oak Point (near today's Rockport) to the old Indian trading grounds, where he and his business partner William Aubrey established a trading post. Kinney called the store and the settlement that took shape on the beach below it Kinney's Rancho but by 1841 he and others were calling it Corpus Christi, after the bay.

The founding of Corpus Christi had a distant connection to the old Santa Fe Trail, which ran from St. Louis and Independence to Santa Fe and northern Mexico. Immense fortunes were made on this great trade route, valued in the 1830s (computed in today's dollars) at $150 million a year. Merchants in New Orleans sought entry into this market of northern Mexico and hired forwarding agents along the Texas coast. Several coastal towns, including Corpus Christi, started as a site where small boats could land contraband cargo for transport inland.

Henry Kinney established Corpus Christi as an outpost for this lucrative Mexican trade. Besides Kinney and William Aubrey, other traders in the settlement included William Mann, Henry Redmond, John P. Kelsey, Frederick Belden, Henry Gilpin, J. R. Everitt and others. Traders from Mexico arrived with trains of pack mules and ox-carts, bringing wool, hides, goat skins and crude silver bars. The wool and hides were sold and proceeds used to buy tobacco, domestic cloth, and manufactured articles for sale back in Mexico. Profits were made coming and going.

This commercial traffic to Chihuahua, Coahuila, and Nuevo León kept schooners sailing between Corpus Christi and New Orleans. This was the economic pulse of Corpus Christi at the time of the arrival of Taylor's army.

Corpus Christi was at the limits of the frontier, located on the edge of disputed territory between the Nueces and Rio Grande, claimed by the Mexico and the Republic of Texas. It was the capital of no man's land.

William Kennedy, the British consul at Galveston, wrote a dispatch saying that Corpus Christi was important as a Texas trading post, "which Mexican contrabandists resort to for the purpose of smuggling goods across the Rio Grande."

Kinney maintained friendly contacts with both sides, writing letters to Mirabeau Lamar, president of the Republic of Texas, and to his friend Gen. Mariano Arista in Matamoros.[*]

In May 1844, the year before the arrival of Taylor's troops, a Comanche raiding party attacked the settlement and in a brief fight a man named Louis Cooke was shot in the temple, costing him an eye. Three days later, the Comanches returned, but the residents were expecting them. Kinney and 11 other men chased them 10 miles west of the settlement, where both sides dismounted for the battle.

When the man-to-man fighting was over, one man was killed (George Gleason) along with two unidentified Hispanics. Kinney, H. W. Berry, and Francisco Silva were wounded. After this attack, Kinney appealed to Austin and was authorized to raise a company of 40 men for the protection of Corpus Christi.

In 1844, Kinney was elected to the Senate of the Ninth Congress of the Republic, representing San Patricio, Goliad and Refugio counties. He voted to ratify the terms of annexation and in 1845 wrote letters to U.S. officials recommending Corpus Christi as a good place to concentrate U.S. troops in the event of trouble with Mexico.

Dating from the time that Kinney established his trading post, in the fall of 1839, Corpus Christi was six years old when Zachary Taylor's army arrived and began setting up camp in the first week of August 1845.

The first companies in Corpus Christi, from Hitchcock's 3rd Regiment, landed supplies on the first day of August. The bay that caused them so much trouble the day before was still rough, the surf cutting up high, so it was difficult

_____

[*] Matamoros, Spanish for "slayer of Moors," was generally spelled Matamoras by American soldiers in the Mexican War.

to land supplies from the small boats. They put up tents, looked for water, and killed rattlesnakes buzzing in the salt grass flats of North Beach.

The companies of the 3rd Infantry were camped on the lower edge of the shoreline with rising bluffs behind them to the south and west. A mile to the west of the encampment was the Nueces River. One wrote that, "This is a pretty spot with a fine bay." Another wrote that, looking from his tent to the east, the sight stretched across Corpus Christi Bay until it reached the horizon. Turning to the southeast, a point of highland (Three Mile Point) jutted into the bay. To the west were high bluffs a few miles from the camp. The highlands were covered with a brush called chaparral.

"For the first time," Lt. W. S. Henry wrote, "I saw the mesquite. It resembles very much the wild locust and bears a bean having a delightfully sweet taste."

One soldier said Corpus Christi was a small village built around a trading post on the edge of Corpus Christi Bay. Another called it "a Mexican hamlet" and said it would have been a wide spot on the road, if there had been a road.

The soldiers were not impressed by the village. One called it "the most murderous, thieving, gambling, God-forsaken hole in the Lone Star State, or out of it." Many considered it part of Mexico. One officer wrote that "We are over the line in Mexico, and ready for anything."

The officers explored their new surroundings and found many Mexican (Hispanic Tejano) families living on the high bluff. "Their residences are made of crooked mesquite wood and their roofs thatched with long grass which grows in the marshes called tula." Some officers were invited to dine at the home of merchant Frederick Belden and his wife Mauricia (Arocha). Lt. Henry said they were given a dish he called "themales." "It is made of corn meal, chopped meat, and cayenne pepper wrapped in a piece of corn husk and boiled. I know of nothing more palatable."

Henry's host, Frederick Belden, had moved to Corpus Christi soon after it was founded. He was in business in Matamoros where he married Mauricia Arocha. Much later, after the army was fully concentrated in Corpus Christi, Frederick and Mauricia held a dinner party for Gen. Taylor and some of his officers. At the dinner Mauricia asked the general about the prospects for war and Taylor said that if war did break out that he intended to march on Mexico City. Mrs. Belden said he would never get there, that he would be crushed if he tried. Taylor didn't capture Mexico City — Winfield Scott did — but he did send Mrs. Belden a silk dress from Mexico.

On Aug. 8, a week after the troops landed, Lt. Henry said the wind blew "a perfect hurricane and it was with great difficulty that our tents could be kept standing. Our camp-ground is infested with rattlesnakes; as many as two at a time have been found in the tents of the officers."

Military order began to emerge. Tents stretched across the mud slough toward the small village. Gen. Taylor and his staff, who moved his headquarters from St. Joseph's on Aug. 15, issued his first order from Corpus Christi. The heading showed he was no longer calling it the Army of Observation. It had become the Army of Occupation.

The schooner Swallow, loaded with baggage and stores, wrecked on the bar. The vessel had no pilot on board and was trying to follow in the wake of the steamboat Monmouth when the current in the pass "swept her into the breakers on the eastern shore of the island," reported the "Daily Picayune" in New Orleans. W. S. Henry said "an immense mail" was thoroughly soaked and mostly ruined. Within a week of the wreck, the Swallow was stripped of its masts, sails and rigging and some of the cargo was saved. A wreck sale was held on Aug. 22.

Other steamboats and schooners under contract to the government for ferrying men and supplies from the large and growing depot on St. Joseph's to Corpus Christi included the Neva, White Wing, Sarah Foyle, Mary Wilkes, E. S. Lamdin, and Monmouth. The army's hired lighter Undine tried to ferry soldiers from St. Joseph's Island but drew too much water to cross over the mudflats. The Undine was replaced by the Dayton, an old steamer that once ran on the Ohio River.

Surgeon N. S. Jarvis and his "sick and hospital stores" were ferried on the Monmouth from the depot to the encampment on Aug. 14. The army's general hospital was established in a building* rented from Kinney along the waterfront (later Water Street) under the charge of surgeon Jarvis.

Other units continued to arrive and the army settled into the routine of soldiering. The troops were kept busy with drills and marching "and your ears are filled all day with drumming and fifeing." The soldiers spent a lot of time on target practice. One officer wrote that, "the Mexican Army being largely composed of cavalry, and a collision being more than probable, our infantry was constantly drilled in forming square to resist cavalry." Another wrote, "We have been firing ball cartridges at targets. And in almost every instance, at a hundred paces, the targets fall shattered to the ground."

The soldiers in Taylor's army were mostly armed with flintlock muskets while some carried .54 caliber rifles. The dragoons were armed with musketoons* carried on sling belts and Prussian-style sabers and horse pistols.

THE SOLDIERS DUG wells, including one at what would be called Artesian Park, but the water had an unpleasant taste and smelled like rotten eggs. The village's drinking

---

* This building was believed to be what was later known as the old Byington house. It was used for the general hospital and offices for some of Taylor's staff. It was torn down in 1910.
* A short-barreled shotgun-like weapon used by cavalry.

water came from "Kinney's Tank," a dam built across a deep ravine that supplied the people with "a plentiful supply of rainwater." But it was not enough for the army. For drinking and cooking, army teamsters hauled water in wooden casks from the Nueces River upstream and it was still considered unhealthy. "Our water is poor," wrote one officer, "and we are made sick by its use."

One problem was the men's refusal to boil their drinking water and another was that military guidelines for setting up a campsite (called "castramentation") was not followed. Training called for choosing a campsite on high ground, with good drainage, with sanitation trenches on lower ground, and the camp within easy reach of wood and water. "Fort Marcy" violated these rules and at least one historian, Holman Hamilton, said Taylor was patently culpable:

> Even in an age when medical science was still in its infancy, sanitary conditions could scarcely have been more primitive than they were in the Corpus Christi camp. That Taylor tolerated a complete lack of sanitation certainly did him little credit. Few soldiers died from disease, but the record shows that diarrhea and dysentery kept an average of ten per cent of the officers and 13 per cent of the men bedridden throughout the late autumn and winter months. Actually, in November and December at least, the number of those affected was even larger.

Another historian, Bernard DeVoto, wrote that Taylor's troops at Corpus Christi "drank bad water and sickened; they drank bad whiskey and brawled. Their rations gave them scurvy, the food they bought from sutlers and Mexicans gave them dysentery."

CHAPTER 6

A Perfectly Awful Storm

In the third week of August, a caravan of Mexican traders arrived from Camargo, across the Rio Grande, with horses, mules and specie. Surgeon N. S. Jarvis noted that bodies of these traders "are constantly arriving and a contraband trade of large amount is carried on between them and the merchants of Corpus Christi. They bring horses, mules, specie, bullion, and Mexican blankets. They buy tobacco, gunpowder, prints and domestic cloths. All this they smuggle across the border. The horses they bring are mostly wild horses, immense herds of which roam the prairie. The prices they sell these for vary from five to 10 dollars. They are generally small and shaggy, wild and unbroken, but hardy and enduring."

The Camargo traders, Col. Hitchcock wrote, brought silver bars, molded in sand, worth $50 to $60 each, which were traded for bales of leaf tobacco, calico cloth and other goods. In his diary, Hitchcock wrote:

> Several of the officers among us went to town and saw various new things. These traders came here with specie mostly and buy tobacco and American goods, cottons, etc. There were sundry curious things among these traders. Their ponchos or traveling blankets — from 10 to 40 dollars price — are of unsurpassed beauty. They are brightly

colored and expertly woven of wool and said to be waterproof. There is a hole in the center for the head and the blanket falls all around one, making a complete protection against rain. Then there is an apparatus (God knows what the name is) made of goatskins, highly ornamented. Two are attached to the saddle bow and hang down so as to cover the traveler's legs and feet. These keep off rain and protect the rider against chaparral bushes and help to make a good bed at night, for the skins are used with the hair on. I saw some of them preparing the goods they had purchased and that too was a sight. The whole thing is a business, a science.

Henry Kinney returned from Austin on Aug. 21, with his escort of several Lipan-Apache Indians for protection. Surgeon Jarvis was amused by a conversation with one of the Indians. "On alluding to their probable connection or relation to Comanches," Jarvis wrote, "he probably understood me, for he immediately and warmly asserted in Spanish that they belonged to no other tribe, and to convince us that no such connection existed with the Comanches, he told us that he had once killed a Comanche warrior, two women, and eat a baby. Under the impression that we may have misunderstood him, as to the last particular, we repeated the inquiry, if such was the fact, which he again reiterated, adding that it was good."

One of the Lipans had "a pair of leggings I would have liked to have got," wrote one officer, and another fellow "had his navel painted vermilion with black around it. They are a bold set of fellows, but their tribe is small. The Comanches are the sovereigns of the prairies of Texas."

Not long after Kinney and his escort arrived, Lipan chief Castro was shot in the head and chest one night. An officer said the wounds he sustained were enough to kill half a dozen men. "Some rascal got him out in the dark to take a drink and then drew a six-barreled pistol and shot the chief in the forehead. He fell, but the ball did not penetrate (the brain). He was shot again in the breast, when miraculously again the ball struck a rib and instead of penetrating traversed around and came out the back. He then got up and ran, when the ruffian (shot) him in the neck and shoulders with a load of buckshot."

Suspicion fell on Louis P. Cooke, who had lost an eye to a Comanche arrow in the raid the year before. Cooke was questioned about the shooting but denied any involvement and there was no evidence to charge him. He was one of several men in Corpus Christi with a troubled past, men who had run away from something or someone.

Cooke was a West Point dropout who became the secretary of the Texas Navy. He was a soldier, legislator, and a murder suspect on the run. He was born in 1811 in Tennessee. He entered West Point in 1833 and left the academy in 1836 to join New York volunteers bound for Texas to fight in the revolution. Somewhere between West Point and Texas he changed his name from John Lane Cooke to Louis P. Cooke.

The New Yorkers arrived too late to take part in the battle of San Jacinto, but Cooke was elected lieutenant colonel in the Texas Army then elected to the Third Congress of the Republic, from Brazoria. He was appointed secretary of the Texas Navy and held that post from 1839 to 1841. Cooke got into trouble in July 1843 when he killed a man in a shooting affray in Austin and was indicted for murder. As his case was scheduled to come to trial, he escaped and made his way to Corpus Christi, taking with him his wife and children. He was working as a bricklayer when the army landed.

Men like Cooke gave the small settlement an unsavory reputation. Lt. Abner Doubleday wrote that Corpus Christi must have been a charming place for people who disliked the restraints of civilization. Lt. Charles May of the dragoons was invited to dine at Cooke's house and Doubleday wrote that:

> May found a motley crowd assembled who were probably all fugitives from justice. Each man ate in silence with his revolver handy and a double-barrel shotgun between his legs. One of the men took offense at something May said and snapped his pistol twice at him but the percussion cap did not go off. Other parties interfered, the assailant was convinced of his error and duly apologized, but May became taciturn for the remainder of the dinner and needless to say was glad when the festivities were over.

"Before our arrival," said Doubleday, "there was no law there but that of the Bowie knife and pistol. In fact, most of the inhabitants had fled in the first place from the United States to Texas on account of the crimes they had committed. One of our officers remarked to me one day, 'Isn't it strange that every gentleman to whom I have been introduced here has murdered somebody?'

Another who went to a barbershop, which had been opened for the accommodation of the army, heard a man remark, 'Has Tom got even with Bill yet?' The other replied, 'Tom hasn't a lick of sense. He fired at Bill, right in the midst of a crowd of people, missed him, then broke and ran for the chaparral. He might have waylaid him in 50 places on his way home, but now he won't have much chance.' "

Aug. 23 was a day of heavy heat with the feeling of unease and portent that comes before a storm. Gen. Taylor and an entourage left to ride to San Patricio to meet Twiggs' Dragoons who had traveled overland from Fort Jesup. Those riding with Taylor included his adjutant, Capt. (Perfect) Bliss, his aide-de-camp, Lt. Joseph Eaton, aide Lt.

Stephen Dobbins, three mounted soldiers, and a guide, Col. Cooke, who seemed to be always on hand. As he usually was, Taylor was dressed not in his military uniform but for comfort, *"like an old farmer going to market with eggs to sell."*

Hitchcock and Henry Kinney rode part of the way with Taylor and on the ride back Kinney told Hitchcock something of his life and adventures. "Kinney is a young man for his experiences, not over 35, and yet he has had incidents enough in his life to make histories of a dozen men. There was no ostentation in his narrative, though I could see that he was sensible enough of the peculiar life he has had. It appears he came here to establish a trading place in 1839."

The Mexican government, Kinney told Hitchcock, imposed such heavy duties on tobacco and other American products that an illicit trade was encouraged. This trade was carried on between Mexicans beyond the Rio Grande. "Kinney must have seen that this place afforded greater facilities for the trade, being nearer the Rio Grande and there being access to it by sea from New Orleans.

"Among the incidents Col. Kinney stated to me are the following, but without regard to order in time. Gov. Sam Houston employed him as a secret agent to Mexico to bring about a peace or armistice, perhaps in 1842. He had been in Mexico, spoke the language and had many friends in that country. While negotiating, but not known as the agent of Houston, a Texas paper fell into the hands of the Mexican authorities alluding to him as an agent of Houston and at the same time a letter from him to Houston was intercepted. He was arrested, sentenced to be shot, led out blindfolded, and the execution squad paraded before him. He escaped by a bribe administered by a friend and trader of Matamoros."

The next day was an overcast and stormy morning when the encampment was hit by a violent thunderstorm. W. S. Henry said the storm was perfectly awful; "it would take your breath away, and make you sit bolt upright in your chair, feet on the rung, as if your life depended on it." A lightning bolt hit a tent center pole, killing a slave* owned by Lt. Braxton Bragg, and injuring another slave in the same tent. It was said the air in the tent smelled like sulfur. "The one killed," N. S. Jarvis wrote, "was sitting in his tent with his head leaning against the tent pole, the top of which the lightning struck." During the storm a baby was born to a laundry woman and Henry thought that it should have been named "Thunder."

Corporal C. M. Reeves said he had never seen such thunderstorms before. "A sentinel walking his post with fixed bayonet was struck, his musket broken, the barrel twisted like an augur, and, strange to say, the man was not killed."

From a distance, the rumbling echo of the thunder was so regular it sounded like artillery. Twiggs' dragoons had marched overland to Texas and were on the last leg of their journey from San Antonio to Corpus Christi when they heard the distant rumble. They were camped at San Patricio up the Nueces River, where they had arrived on Aug. 23.

The dragoons thought Taylor's army was being pounded to oblivion by hostile forces from Mexico. They swam their horses across the Nueces and galloped toward Corpus Christi in relief. They met Gen. Taylor and aides coming to greet them.

The dragoons finally arrived at Corpus Christi and began to set up camp on Aug. 27. Twiggs left two companies as an outpost at San Patricio, the old Irish village that was more a name than a place; it had been deserted since the Texas Revolution. After the arrival of the 2nd Dragoons,

---

* In diaries and letters, Taylor's soldiers rarely mention the slaves that accompanied them. When the army moved into Mexico, officers' slaves were close to freedom; some ran away and some were freed by their owners. Taylor set the example by freeing his valet, Bob Thompson, known a Little Bob, who returned to the Corpus Christi to settle down.

Taylor in a report to Washington said Twiggs' troops on their long march crossed the Sabine into Texas, traveled west over open prairies, crossed the Trinity, Brazos, Colorado, San Marcos, Guadalupe, San Antonio, and halted on the west bank of the Nueces at San Patricio. Some of the streams were forded and others crossed by ferry.

Some 50 of the dragoons deserted on the long trip, Hitchcock wrote, mainly because "the backs of the horses became injured and the men were required to lead them, which disgusted them or broke them down." One man died from overexertion then drinking too much cold water and two men died of sunstroke — "*coup de soliel*," noted Hitchcock — soon after they crossed into Texas but there were no casualties after that and Taylor in his report to Washington said the dragoons and their horses "were in excellent condition after this long summer march."*

When Twiggs' command was near San Antonio, they ran into a large party of Comanches (reported to be 300 warriors) and an impromptu peace parley was held. The Comanches "seemed much delighted" at the prospect of war between the United States and Mexico, reported the "Daily Picayune," and the Indians admired the dragoons' horses and joked about stealing them. This was too much for Twiggs, described as "a bull with white whiskers." He said he would hang them if they did, but they were free to steal all the horses they wanted from the Mexican Army.

After Twiggs' arrival, a depot was established on the beach, behind the entrenchments and, wrote Henry, "great activity prevailed in the attempt to purchase mules and cattle for transportation of the army in case of an emergency."

---

* With Twiggs' 2nd Dragoons were two bugle boys, Irish orphans named Matthew and Thomas Nolan, who later became central figures in the early history of Corpus Christi. Matthew was elected sheriff of Nueces County and his brother Thomas was hired as deputy sheriff. Both were killed in the line of duty.

On the following day, the steam packet Alabama arrived off Aransas Pass with three companies of the 7th Regiment of Infantry (Zachary Taylor's own first regiment, where he began his military career as a second lieutenant) followed by two companies of the 4th on board the brig William Ivy.

On the William Ivy's passage from New Orleans, one of the soldiers in a fit of delirium tremens jumped overboard. A boat was lowered and went after him. He resisted being saved, reported the "New Orleans Daily Picayune," but was picked, taken back aboard and tied up. When a squall hit the ship he was released, in case the ship went down, and he again jumped into the water. This time he was lost.

When the lighter transporting the troops got stuck on the mud shoals in Corpus Christi Bay, Lt. Napoleon Jackson Tecumseh Dana wrote his wife Sue that the men got into the waist-deep water to try to tow the vessel off. While they were stuck, Dana took his gun, jumped overboard, and went hunting. He shot two birds for his supper.

Dana's brother-in-law, Capt. Daniel Powers Whiting of the 7th Regiment noted in his diary that:

> We landed at St. Joseph's Island and taking the transport steamer Dayton — an old and unsafe boat which a few days afterward blew up, killing several officers and men — reached Corpus Christi on the 31st of August. We encamped with other troops already there under Gen. Taylor.

As Whiting's company began clearing the scrub-covered ground for a regimental camp, they found, like others before them, that the Rincon was crawling with rattlesnakes. Many were killed. "I was awakened one night by the rattle of one in my tent, close to where I was lying, that had its head outside, alarmed by a dog barking at it. Gathering myself up, I called some men and sprang out. When the snake was killed, I found it to be about six feet in length. These and other vermin that can make life miserable prevailed at the camp. We frequently find scorpions in our clothing and boots when about to put them on."

Whiting's brother-in-law, Lt. Dana, also in the 7th, wrote his wife that "there are a million flies here, thicker than the mosquitoes at Fort Pike. There is at least one in every cup of coffee we drink. Our boiled ham today was basted with dead flies, which had drowned in the fat after it was put on the table. This is a mighty thriving country for cockroaches, too. The blots on this paper, Sue, are a specimen of what the cockroaches do. They get in the inkstand and then crawl over the paper, leaving their tracks behind."

In another letter to his wife, Lt. Dana said they had been hard at work clearing the grounds for the camp. "We have a great deal yet to do, in fact we will continue to have hard work till we go home again, which will be God knows when. I don't think there is anything to be done in the way of fighting. If there is, it will be a long time first. If Mexico declares war, I believe General Taylor means to march us right on Matamoros. If he does, it is to be hoped that we will not get a whipping and get knocked on the head."

After the encampment was cleared, Whiting said, it stood on a fine esplanade. The camp was of some two miles in extent, parallel to the shore of the bay, extending from the village of Corpus Christi to the point of land made by the junction of the Nueces Bay with Corpus Christi Bay." Not long afterwards, Whiting made a sketch of the camp which was afterwards published in his "Army Portfolio." *

---

* Whiting, trained at West Point in topographical drawing, published five lithographs of the Mexican War. His depiction of the army encampment at Corpus Christi, drawn in October 1845, represents the "Bayeux tapestry" of Corpus Christi's history."

CHAPTER 7

Steamboat Dayton Explodes

In the first week of September, the 4th Regiment began to arrive and the troops were ferried to the encampment aboard the sidewheel steamer, the Dayton.

Surgeon N. S. Jarvis noted on Sept. 3 that "a Mexican man was caught in the dragoon camp and charged with an attempt to decoy away slaves, servants of some of the officers. He was immediately put in irons."

Hitchcock went to see Henry Kinney, who was sick, on Sept. 7 and found Gen. Taylor and William Mann, a prominent trader, visiting the town founder. Hitchcock met Kinney's confidante and spy, Chipito Sandoval, who had just ridden in from the Rio Grande with reports of army movements in Mexico. Hitchcock later noted in his diary that Sandoval heard that 3,000 Mexican troops "are approaching Matamoros — will reach there in a week. Now only about 500 men are there. Revolt of Mexicans south of river threatened. We are quite in the dark. The general may have information which he keeps to himself, but I know him too well to believe he has any."

The general's information came from the same source as Hitchcock's, but he put a different interpretation on it. After his meeting with Chipito at Kinney's house, Taylor wrote Washington (the adjutant general) and related that:

A confidential agent (Chipito) dispatched some days before to Matamoros has returned and reports that no extraordinary preparations are going forward there; that the garrison does not seem to have been increased, and that our consul is of opinion there will be no declaration of war. A decree had been issued prohibiting, under penalty of death, any communication, by writing, across the frontier . . . Nothing definite can be learned in relation to the march of troops from the interior. A body of 3,000 men was reported in march to Matamoros, but the information is too vague to merit much confidence. The agent, who is intelligent, and on whose statements a good deal of reliance may, I think, be safely placed, says that the people with whom he mingled are opposed to a war with us and that if war be declared the frontier departments of Tamaulipas, Coahuila, and Nuevo Leon, will probably declare themselves independent of the central government and establish pacific relations with us.

On Sept. 12, the boilers on the steamboat Dayton, exploded while carrying troops to the encampment. Col. Hitchcock wrote in his diary: "Yesterday brought us a disaster. A small old steamer, the Dayton, employed for a few days by the government, burst her boilers a few miles from here, near McGloin's Bluff (Ingleside) and killed seven men and wounded 17. The Dayton had just completed the time for which she was hired when she exploded, with such terrible results."

Lt. Dana wrote his wife that the Dayton was "a miserable apology for a boat," which had once been used to haul wood to Fort Pike in Louisiana, "blew up today just on her way to St. Joseph's Island. The explosion was tremendous and the boat a complete wreck. There were some eight or ten officers on board at the time, two of whom, poor fellows, Lieutenants Higgins and Berry of the 4th were killed and Lt. Richard H. Graham was badly scalded. Among the killed was Corporal Chambers. He had been discharged and was going home. He was mashed to a mummy. Poor Mrs. Higgins.* They had been married but ten days when they were separated. Hers is a hard case. A poor widow and so young. The old craft never ought to have been hired, as she was about 50 years old."

The "Niles National Register" reported the disaster in its Sept. 27, 1845 edition:

"The steamer Dayton when halfway between Corpus Christi and St. Joseph's Island, having between 30 and 40 persons on board, exploded a boiler. Ten persons were killed, including Lieuts. Wiggins (Higgins) and Berry, of the 4th regiment of infantry. Seventeen were wounded, one of whom died next day. Capt. Crosman, quartermaster, was blown to a distance of 100 yards, but next day, though somewhat bruised, was able to walk and attend to business. The boat sank in 15 minutes after the explosion. As she went down, another boiler exploded, with a most terrible report."

Col. Hitchcock picked the burial site on the brow of a hill with a view of Nueces and Corpus Christi bays, "a very beautiful spot." With the light fading at sundown, the 4th Regiment band played the melancholy "Dead March in Saul" by George Frederic Handel. W. S. Henry wrote that the ceremony was impressive:

> The sun had just set; the clouds, piled up in pyramids, were tinged with golden light; flashes of lightning were seen in the north; the pale moon, in the east, was smiling sweetly. The service of the dead was read by the light of a lamp. Three volleys were fired over their graves. The escort wheeled into column and to a lively air from fife

---

* Mrs. Higgins was the daughter of Capt. Morris of the 3rd Infantry.

and drum we left the soldiers to their long sleep. May the God of Battles receive and cherish them.[*]

A DAY LATER, A YOUNG second lieutenant in the 4th Regiment, Ulysses S. Grant, thought he knew how the pulleys worked on the transport ship Suviah and as the soldiers were being transferred to lighters to cross Corpus Christi Bay, Grant jumped on the rail, grabbed a rope, and promptly fell 25 feet, head over heels into the bay.

Being a good swimmer, Grant later wrote, and not having lost his presence of mind, he swam around the ship until he could grab a rope and sailors pulled him back up on deck like wet parcel. Grant thought it a good joke on himself and laughed with everyone else.

Grant soon explored his new surroundings and described Corpus Christi as "a small American trading-post, at which goods were sold to Mexican smugglers. All goods were put up in compact packages of about 100 pounds each, suitable for loading on pack mules. Two of these packages made a load for an ordinary Mexican mule, and three for the larger ones. The bulk of the trade was in leaf-tobacco and domestic cotton cloths and calicoes. The Mexicans had, before the arrival of the army, but little to offer in exchange except silver. The trade in tobacco was enormous, considering the population to be supplied. Almost every Mexican above the age of ten, and many much younger, smoked the cigarette. Nearly every Mexican carried a pouch of leaf-tobacco, powdered by rolling in the hands, and a roll of corn-husks to make wrappers. The cigarettes were made by the smokers as they used them."

It was a summer and fall of troop movements across the country, down the rivers and around the coast to a remote corner of Texas. Other units continued to arrive in

---

[*] These were the first burials in what became Old Bayview Cemetery.

September. Between Sept. 13 and Sept. 24, wrote W. S. Henry, "the following companies of United States troops arrived, viz.: Gen. William J. Worth, with six companies of the 8th Infantry; Major Samuel Ringgold, with his company of Horse Artillery of the 3rd; two companies of the 8th under Captain Ogden; also Lt. Duncan's company and battery. Add to these Capt. Burke's command (artillery), and five companies of the 5th Infantry under Capt. Smith.

"These latter-named troops have made a prompt and exceedingly rapid movement," said Henry. "They traveled 2,500 miles in 21 days. Detroit was their starting-point; thence across to the Ohio River by canal; down the Ohio and Mississippi in steamboats to New Orleans, and by the fast steam packet Alabama to Aransas Bay.

"A movement of this kind brings into bold relief our grand system of internal navigation, which, in connection with our rivers, enables the government, in an incredibly short period, to send troops from one extremity of the Union to the other."

"When we arrived at Aransas Pass," wrote Lt. Samuel G. French, an officer in Maj. Samuel Ringgold's battery of horse artillery, part of the 3rd Artillery, "the sea was high and the wind was strong and no lighters would venture outside to come to us.

"The discharging of the cargo was tedious, as the horses had to be swung to the yardarms and lowered into the pitching tugs alongside. I had been 46 days on board ship and joyous was it to be landed on St. Joseph's Island."

Some days later, they were transported to Corpus Christi on a lighter which anchored a mile from shore and the 150 horses of the company "were thrown overboard and made to swim to land," French wrote.

On Sept. 18, a scouting expedition left the encampment to travel up the Nueces River in five Mackinaw boats.[*] Lt. George Gordon Meade, a topographical engineer, was on the expedition. In a letter to his wife Meade wrote that they left the main encampment and proceeded into a large bay (the Nueces) and went in search of the river:

> Being ignorant of the country, we missed the mouth of the river, and the first night out was spent by some of the men in their boats; but I was lucky in finding a good place ashore to camp, where, being joined by one of the boats loaded with provisions, I pitched my tent, had a good supper that night, and breakfast next morning.
>
> The next day we made another ineffectual attempt to ascend the river, and got into a bayou, which led us into lakes, and then into other bayous till, finally, we reached a lake having so little water we could advance no farther.
>
> Under these circumstances we camped for the night and the next morning early I was sent out with four men to explore the country around, and ascertain if the river was in our neighborhood. A few miles traveling brought me to the stream which debouched into the bay, about its middle, instead of its head. I returned, set the party on the right road, which obliged us to retrace our steps, and the third day out we encamped on the banks of the Nueces.
>
> After getting into the river we had comparatively easy work. We ordinarily arose at daybreak, had breakfast, took down our tents, loaded the boats, and by seven o'clock were on the way . . . During

---

[*] The army's Mackinaw (sic) boats were light-draft sailboats that originated around the Mackinac Straits on Lake Michigan.

the day, and after we halted, some of the men would take their muskets and go along the banks and were always sure to bring in some wild turkeys, very delicious birds.

It took us four days to ascend the river, when we arrived at what was once the town of San Patricio, now in ruins and deserted. This place was settled by almost 300 Irish emigrants, under the protection of the Mexican government; but during the war that devastated this country, it was a prey to both parties and now there is not one stone standing on another. We stayed at here two days, and arrived three days later at the main camp.

On Sept. 20, Gen. Taylor visited Col. Hitchcock in his tent for a meeting and broached the topic of moving the army to the Rio Grande. Hitchcock told him that if he suggested such a movement President James K. Polk would seize upon it and use it for his ends, to provoke a war.

Said Hitchcock: "I discovered this time more clearly than ever that the general is instigated by ambition — or so it appears to me. He seems quite to have lost all respect for Mexican rights and willing to be an instrument of Mr. Polk for pushing our boundary as far west as possible."

"When I told him that if he suggested a movement (which he told me he intended), Mr. Polk would seize upon it and throw the responsibility on him, he at once said he would take it, and added that if the president instructed him to use his discretion, he would ask no orders, but would go upon the Rio Grande as soon as he could get transportation. I think the general wants an additional brevet* and would strain a point to get it."

---

* Taylor would soon receive it. He was promoted to Brevet Major General after the battles of Palo Alto and Resaca de la Palma on May 8 and May 9, 1846.

CHAPTER 8

Quite a Dangerous Crowd

Zachary Taylor's army continued to concentrate — a tide of men flooding in by water — with the arrival of additional units. The camp stretched from North Beach almost to the town of Corpus Christi two miles away. Looking toward the bluff from the bay, on the far right on North Beach, or Rincon, was the 1st Brigade under Gen. William J. Worth, composed of the 8th Infantry and 12 companies of artillery.

To Gen. Worth's left, closer to the town, was Col. David E. Twiggs' 2nd Dragoons followed by the 2nd Brigade, composed of the 5th and 7th regiments of infantry, under the command of Lt. Col. James S. McIntosh, called "Old Tosh" by the troops.

After the 2nd Brigade was a command of horse artillery under Maj. John Erving. Then the 3rd Brigade, composed of the 3rd and 4th Infantry, commanded by Col. William Whistler (appointed to the vacancy after the death of Col. Vose) and two companies of volunteer artillery from New Orleans.

In all, the army was composed of 3,900 men — "quite a dangerous crowd to fall in with," wrote Lt. W. S. Henry. It was the U.S. largest army assembled in one place since the American Revolution. The "Niles National Register" noted that this large concentration of U. S. troops was now located "beyond what was very recently the bounds of the Union."

To the west of the camp, on the outer perimeter, were the Texas Rangers under the command of John Coffee Hays. The Rangers had been mustered into U.S. service under the authority of Gen. Taylor. While Hays was respected by the army officers for his reputation as a fearless Indian fighter, regular officers didn't think much of the uncouth-looking Rangers.

Lt. Napoleon Jackson Tecumseh Dana wrote that "the best of them looked like they could steal sheep." For their part, the Rangers — insouciant and boastful and undisciplined when not in a fight — teased the regulars by claiming they had arrived, in case of any hostile moves from Mexico, to protect the army.

Historian T. R. Fehrenbach ("Lone Star") wrote that Hays' Rangers, when they arrived at the encampment, were not in any sort of uniform but were well-mounted and doubly well-armed; each man carried one or two Colt revolvers. "The Mexicans are terribly afraid of them."

James Love of Galveston, who visited Corpus Christi during that time, wrote that the Rangers were teaching the regular soldiers how to ride. "The feats of horsemanship of our frontiersmen are most extraordinary. I saw one of them pick up from the ground three dollars, each 50 yards apart, at full speed, and pass under the horse's neck at a pace not much short of full speed."

One of the Rangers at Corpus Christi famous for his skills on horseback was Mabry 'Mustang' Gray. Gray's feat, like that described by Love, was to pick up a Mexican dollar in the street while in full gallop. During the war to come, his company of Rangers would become infamous for committing a cold-blooded massacre of innocent civilians in Mexico.

In a letter to his wife, Lt. Dana said he had heard that a lady had arrived at St. Joseph's. "Who, I do not know. Poor thing. She will really be in a very bad fix indeed. I expect she will pretty soon find her way back to Orleans. I presume she came over from one of the Florida posts. She will find this a worst place than Florida. Here we are in the field, in the true meaning of the word, living real soldiers' lives, and a lady can find nothing comfortable here."

It turned out to be the wife of army surgeon Hamilton S. Hawkins, assigned to the 1st Brigade. Dana's brother-in-law, Capt. Daniel P. Whiting, wrote in his diary that Mrs. Hawkins was "quite a belle, attracting a levee of visitors by day and serenaders by night."

Dana, however, was not one of them. But he did seem obsessed by her presence in the camp. In another letter to his wife, he wrote, "Think, dearest, what a time Mrs. Hawkins is having of it here in camp. This wet weather. It must be exceedingly disagreeable for her . . . It is certainly very annoying to officers in the field to have a lady in camp near them and then it is so very public for her. No privacy whatsoever." He writes that Gen. Taylor had remonstrated with her, saying, 'Well, madam, we did not expect any ladies, but since you are here we will make you as comfortable as we can, but if you had come with the command, you would not have started, I can tell you.' "

In another letter on Oct. 6, Dana wrote, "I saw Mrs. Hawkins ride through camp in a two-horse buggy wagon with an officer. I hear nothing of her but I know that she cannot be made comfortable in a place such as this . . . She has no children, I believe, in fact, if she had, she would not be here, I expect, for camp is no place to bring young children to. Still less is it a place to have them in."

IN OCTOBER, SOLDIERS were ordered to a flat tableland a mile west of the camp, on the bluff, to clear ground for drills. They had been drilling by regiments and brigades, but this larger area would allow the whole army to be drilled together. Lt. Dana said, "It will be the largest scale our army has performed on for many years."

If they could perform, which Col. Hitchcock very much doubted. "What a pretty figure we cut here," he wrote in his diary. "We have the 3rd, 4th and 7th regiments of infantry, the 2nd regiment of dragoons, a company of regular artillery, and among senior officers (except for himself), neither Gen. Taylor nor Col. Whistler commanding the brigade could form them into line. Even Col. Twiggs could put the troops into line only after a fashion of his own." *
Hitchcock did not say so, but clearly conveyed the thought that Taylor was lucky to have such a man as himself in command of one of his regiments.

Lt. Jeremiah Scarritt, an engineer, and a party of soldiers were put to work cutting through the reef that divided Nueces and Corpus Christi Bays (and which later served as the underwater reef road). This cut in the reef on the Corpus Christi side would allow small boats to cross into Nueces Bay and travel up the Nueces River to ferry supplies to the village of San Patricio, where Col. Twiggs had stationed an outpost of dragoons.

During the pleasant days of October, some of the men slept outside their tents on beds of straw. Dana wrote his wife that Col. Twiggs told them that sleeping on the ground out in the open "was never intended for gentlemen, but for blackguards."

Soldiers found that wild mustang horses were cheap. Lt. Grant, a fine rider who loved horses, bought four mustang ponies. A man named Valere, a hired servant (a free black man from Louisiana), was taking Grant's horses to water and let them get away. Capt. W. W. (Perfect) Bliss, Taylor's adjutant, joked, "I heard that Lt. Grant lost five or six dollars' worth of horses the other day."

---

* Three of the colonels in command of troops under Taylor at Corpus Christi, William G. Belknap, J. S. McIntosh, and William Whistler, said one historian, "were ready to fight in 1845 as they had fought in the war of 1812."

There was another story about Grant and a horse. Grant, though he was engaged to Miss Julia Dent back in Missouri, took a young lady named Elizabeth Moore out riding. Henry W. Berry, one of Kinney's hired gun hands and a bricklayer in the town, was also courting Miss Moore. Berry would later tell the story that:

> I had a very handsome and docile little mare which Lt. Grant and other officers would borrow to take Miss Moore out riding. She was afraid of the government horses, which were large and spirited. This horse-loaning business got to be monotonous and I put a stop to it. Lt. Grant was miffed about it and soon my little mare was missing. Sometime afterwards, I was in company with Col. Cooke and we were riding by where the government horses were kept, when he said to me, "Captain, there is your little mare." I said I guessed not. "Yes, it is," said Cooke. "I turned and looked again and sure enough, there she was. Her mane and tail had been shaved. It was a trick of Grant's. I went to Gen. Twiggs and complained. The general seemed surprised. He said he had supposed the animal belonged to them, that it was Lt. Grant who turned her in.

The men spent a lot of time buying and selling horses or racing horses. Sgt. Major Charles Masland in a letter to his brother wrote, "I bought a good pony for a dollar-fifty and saw another swapped for an old pair of soldier's trousers."

Soldiers found amusement in betting on Mexican ponies that were trained to stop instantly on the slightest touch of the reins, wrote Lt. Samuel G. French. "A line would be marked in the sand on the seashore and the rider of the pony would take all bets that he could run his pony a hundred yards at full speed and stop him instantly within a foot of the line, and not pass over it; and they generally won the bets."

Lt. French said he was offered a horse and saddle for $75 — which was $70 for the saddle and $5 for the horse. He bought a hunting pony for $15, which turned out to be "the best trained hunting pony I ever knew. The owner proclaimed that he was *mucho bueno* for hunting, and so he proved to be. At full speed he was trained to stop instantly the moment a motion was made to fire the gun. He loved the smell of gunpowder better than I did."

French said there were fast horses and racing was a daily occurrence. "On one occasion the officers got up a grand race, Capt. Charles May[*] (of the 2nd Dragoons) and Lt. Randolph Ridgely (of the 3rd Artillery) were to ride the respective horses. When mounted. May's feet nearly reached the ground; and they rode bareback. It was an exciting race. On they came under whip and spur amidst the crowd shouting wild hurrah. As they crossed the goal, May thoughtlessly checked his pony, and instantly the animal straightened his forelegs and stopped, but May. Not having braced himself, went on. Seizing the pony by the neck with both hands, his legs rose in the air and he made a complete somersault, landing on the ground some 12 feet in front of the pony. As he was not injured, the crowd went wild with joy."

Lt. Henry went for a ride on a mustang, complete with Mexican rigging. "The animal was lively and frisky enough," he wrote, "but a mere rat compared with our large northern horses."

Almost every day for a month, Henry wrote, some kind of race was held. He described one race, for 300 yards, between two mustang ponies. "One pony bolted, and, not at

---

[*] Capt. May stood 6-4 "without his boots on" and wore his hair and beard long. The men in his company adopted the same fashion of having beards and long hair.

all alarmed by the crowd, cleared two or three piles of rubbish, knocked one man down, threw his rider, ran about 50 yards, stopped, turned around, and snorted — as much as to say, 'Beat that if you can.' "

One day, said Henry, a party of Mexican mustangers brought in a horse reputed to be the celebrated "White Horse of the Prairies" so often described by travelers. "He was a flea-bitten gray, 14 hands high, well-proportioned, and built a good deal after the pattern of a Conestago No. 2. His head and neck were beautiful, perfect Arabian; beautiful ears, large nostrils, great breadth of forehead, and a throttle as large as any I have ever seen in a blooded nag. His white mane was two feet long. He looked about 25 years old. He was driven into a pen with some 100 others. Thus, by an artifice, was entrapped the monarch of the mustangs. No more will he lead the countless herds in their wild scampers of freedom; no more will be seen his noble form, with head up and eye dilated, standing on the prairie-knoll, snuffing danger in the breeze, and dashing off at lightning-speed when it becomes apparent."

On Oct. 13, the steamer Alabama brought from New Orleans five companies of the 5th regiment, Hitchcock noted, "so that now all of the troops ordered to this place by President Polk have arrived."

A GROUP OF SOLDIERS ON a three-day hunting trip to the Nueces River bottoms killed deer, geese and a seven-foot panther that sprang at Lt. Stephen Dobbins, missed, and when he tried another leap the lieutenant shot him in the head. "No one but the most irreclaimable cynic," wrote Henry, "could have ridden over this beautiful country, in the vicinity of the Nueces, without being enchanted with its beauty."

Sgt. Masland agreed. In a letter to his brother in Lowell, Mass., he wrote that he was out "gunning" on the banks of the Nueces and "never did I see such picturesque and delightful scenery in my life. Imagine to yourself a view as far as the eye can see of rolling prairie, relieved here and there by natural groves, covered with rich luxuriant grasses and flowers everywhere with the colors of the rainbow, with game, such as wild geese and deer in great abundance. It is decidedly a fine country, a paradise."

During an interval of fine weather, another hunting party traveled up the Nueces River. Capt. George A. McCall of the 4th Regiment said it consisted of himself and Col. John Garland, his commanding officer; Capt. Martin Scott and Lt. Randolph Marcy of the 5th Regiment. McCall wrote that:

> Col. Garland and I had a five-mule team and wagon for our tents, baggage, and provisions. Scott and Marcy had another. We also had four soldiers to each wagon as a guard against Indians. The four with our wagon were of my own company; those of the other wagon were of Scott's company, and with the teamsters (also soldiers and armed) and ourselves, made a party of 14 well-armed hunters.
>
> We marched about 70 miles up the Nueces River and hunted there three days. The result was some 20 deer, about 70 turkeys, and ducks, geese, and partridges not numbered. Most of the game succumbed to Marcy and myself, but two or three of the deer having been shot by the other officers. Of the turkeys, all but two were fine gobblers, and in the most brilliant plumage, as well as in condition for the table. We had quite a pleasant time, the weather being as fine as one could desire.

CHAPTER 9

Heavy Rain and Cold Comfort

Before the army's arrival the village of Corpus Christi counted less than 100 in population. Within two months, the numbers had grown to more than a thousand people as the town filled with those who saw the army as an opportunity. There were adventurers, gamblers, saloon-keepers, prostitutes — all looking to profit from the 4,000-man army camped by the town. In Hitchcock's description:

> Corpus Christi, commencing at the south extremity, presents first the house where Col. Kinney had his store. It is now rented by the U.S. for a hospital. Next door is Mr. Mann's establishment, then a lagoon, followed by an eating house for loafers, a bake shop (Conrad Meuly's), Owens' store, smaller huts for drinking, a two-story house rented by the U.S. for hospital purposes, a cluster of drinking houses, perhaps a dozen, all put up since our arrival and presenting a very odd appearance; the first named houses are mostly in one line along the shore, but north of the last hospital the huts spread out without much regularity and some of them are made by a light framework sawed out of common boards and nailed together and covered with course cotton

cloth, anything for a sort of shelter under which liquor may be sold.

Houses appear to have been built in a night, Lt. W. S. Henry wrote. "There are all sorts, from a frame covered with common domestic (cloth), to a tolerably respectable one, clap-boarded and shingled." One building being erected in November was a theater — "of no inconsiderable dimensions," said Henry.

Edward Jay Nichols in "Zach Taylor's Little Army" described Kinney's settlement after the army settled in:

Surgeon N. S. Jarvis took over one of the few frame buildings for a hospital and medical storehouse, with guard; whiskey was a popular remedy. Ordnance, commissary, and subsistence arranged for supply depots. Wheelwrights threw up sheds for repairing wagons and gun carriages; blacksmiths whanged away in areas of their own; corrals for the horses, mules, and oxen sprawled over acres; and artillery and wagon parks elbowed for extra space. The slaughtering pens lay beyond camp. Add the parade ground, and Taylor's war machine had eaten up miles of landscape.

A job-seeker from New Orleans named Josiah Turner arrived to look for work in the new boomtown. He stayed at a hotel on Chaparral, a one-story frame structure built and run by a man named Moore.

"That was the only hotel in Corpus Christi and it was not yet completed, and without furniture," Turner wrote. "A cold norther sprang up and I had to make up bed on a pile of shavings. It was lucky I had a pair of Mackinaw blankets which kept me from freezing. I thought it was coldest country I ever saw.

"As I had only $25 left after paying passage, I tried to get employment as a clerk in some of the stores, but not being able to speak Spanish I did not succeed. There were many temporary houses being constructed with modern frame walls covered with domestic sheeting, for saloons and different purposes; some were for drinking and some for gambling, and others for restaurants. As I had learned from Uncle Jim, my mother's carpenter, how to drive nails and saw wood straight, and mechanics being in demand, I earned my five dollars a week at the carpenter's trade.

"Gen. Taylor's army was camped a little above where the courthouse is now situated. I used to enjoy going to the heights every evening at retreat to hear the band of Gen. Worth's 8th Regiment under the leadership of Mr. Roca play. The recollection of the setting sun on the bay, blended with the music, presented the most beautiful and enchanting scene and atmosphere I ever beheld."

Others were not so enchanted.

"When we came here," Sgt. George K. Donnelly wrote home, "the celebrated city of Corpus Christi consisted of about two good frame houses, seven or eight miserable huts, all of which were grog shops or gamblers' dens.[*] Now it has 60 or 70 good houses, about 1,400 inhabitants, but I am sorry to say that more than two-thirds are of the lowest class of villains — men who are reckless of character and human life." Considering its inhabitants, it seemed an unlikely place for its name — Body of Christ.

Not long after the army had arrived, Sgt. Charles Masland wrote to his brother in Lowell, Mass., that the grog shops "reared their hydra heads, and stood with open doors to invite the too easily duped soldiers with gaming tables, ten-pin alleys, hot whisky punch . . . everything that could afford the least attraction to the novelty-seeking

---

[*] Lt. George Gordon Meade called them "groggeries" where soldiers on payday were sure to find a glad hand and overpouring affability.

soldier, and many — alas! too many — surrendered at discretion." Masland said Gen. Taylor had drawn some criticism for not placing the town under martial law and closing down the grog shops and gambling dens.

There were problems, especially with Twiggs' dragoons. Hitchcock noted that there had been several disgraceful brawls in which the dragoons were the instigators. One scrape involved "a low vulgar slut of a strumpet." Hitchcock said Col. Twiggs' regiment was known to have kept women "in prostitution in the tents of the officers, the colonel setting the example."

Hitchcock heard that at one orgy Twiggs got drunk and as they sang obscene songs had liquor ("agua fortis") poured over his naked body. The commander of the dragoons, said Hitchcock, was an example of depravity, "a hoary-headed old lecher" known for "licentiousness with women in open defiance of public opinion."

The incident involving agua fortis and dancing girls was revealed in a general court-martial that sat for four days involving a fight between Capt. Croghan Ker and First Lt. Owen P. Ransom of the 2nd Dragoons. Hitchcock said Twiggs' conduct and the "whole character of the regiment" was brought out in evidence and again in the written summary at the close of the trial. Lt. Ransom, found guilty of drunkenness, was dismissed from the service.

CAPT. DANIEL P. WHITING of the 7th Infantry established a "mess" for the officers managed by a laundry woman named Sarah Bourjett from Tennessee, a tall six-foot-three woman of large frame with flaming red hair. She was nominally married to one of the sergeants in Whiting's company.

Whiting said one day he heard a noise in the camp and when he looked up he "saw her pick up a man who had offended her and, as if he were a child, set him down in her wash tub."

64

Because of her size she gained the nickname of the Great Western, after a famous steamship of the day. A "Great Western Eating Salon" — which may have been Sarah's place — advertised in the "Gazette" that it would serve meals to bachelors at any time day or night, with oysters the house specialty.

Later, on the trip to the Rio Grande, she followed along with Whiting's company in a mule cart loaded with supplies for the officers' mess. She became widely known for tending the wounded in the bombardment of Fort Brown and, one officer said, she was in the thick of fighting and a piece of shrapnel tore a hole through her bonnet.

Still later, during the war in Mexico, first in Matamoros then in Monterrey, she opened a place called the American House, described as a boarding house or "sort of a hotel" where the specialty of the house was women for rent by the hour. She opened another "hotel" in Saltillo. During the battle of Buena Vista, a soldier ran into Sarah's place in a panic and yelled that Taylor's army was all cut to pieces by the Mexican army. The Great Western was outraged. She knocked the man down and said, "You son of a bitch, there ain't Mexicans enough in Mexico to whip old Taylor. You spread that rumor and I'll beat you to death."

The Army turned a blind eye to the activities of the laundry women who were sometimes, like the Great Western, in business for themselves. Many were married to enlisted men, which gave them a legal status and allowed them, with a wink and a nod, to ply their trade.

Each company was allowed four laundresses, who drew rations like the men, and the officers fixed their price and deducted their pay, from that of the soldiers. One laundry woman in the 4th Infantry (Lt. Grant's regiment) was described as an ugly muscular Dutch woman, married to a Private Clancy, who "was given to whipping her husband every little while."

At the encampment in Corpus Christi on Nov. 1, Twiggs' dragoons paraded in full dress followed by a review of the Louisiana Volunteer Artillery. The Louisiana Volunteers left the following day for home because their term of enlistment had expired.

In a letter to his wife, Lt. John James Peck wrote that he feared that "we shall remain here all winter and leave in the spring without seeing anything. Nothing would have pleased me more than some skirmishing, for we should have been on the move. But I am young and must wait patiently.

"We have horses, oxen and wagons, and the rainy season is coming on," Lt. Peck wrote. "We have four thousand troops of the best kind, 30 odd pieces of artillery, and the strong desire to go. In addition to this force, the general is authorized to call out 3,000 Texans who are already enrolled. With this force I think we could clear the disputed region of all Mexicans."

Lt. Napoleon Jackson Tecumseh Dana wrote his wife that the tailor John Smith had arrived from New Orleans "and is dunning the officers." Dana said he owed Smith $100 but that he didn't ask him for it. "I had no idea a tailor could have so much delicacy."

Dana's own debt exceeded his ability to pay, as he outlined in a letter to Susan, his wife, with a long-term plan on how he proposed cut their monthly expenses to settle it:

> My expenses this month will not exceed 18 dollars. When I give those men all their money, I shall feel happy indeed. They do not want it now, have not asked for it, but they might. You want me to tell you about the sums? I owe Sgt. Weigart $255; Wise, $69, Armstrong $20, and Burke $65. In all, $409.
>
> Now, at the end of this month, toward paying this, I shall have $60, which leaves a balance due

of $349. That is a pretty big sum, but if we are prudent and economical, we can pay it. Now, if each of us can get along on $18 a month, we can save $30 each month and it will take a year to pay off this debt."

Lt. Augustus Cook of the 2nd Dragoons left the encampment for New Orleans on sick leave. On the way, on Nov. 1, Surgeon N. S. Jarvis said he jumped overboard "in a fit of temporary insanity" and was drowned. Jarvis said he had previously tried to cut his throat in a Galveston hotel. "He was an amiable young officer but had for some time suffered ill health which doubtless affected his mind."

THE WEATHER TURNED COLD and rainy, with the arrival of a norther on Nov. 20. This brought a spell of miserable dripping weather of gray days, with the men peering out from their tent flaps at the incessantly falling rain.

The whole encampment was mired in mud and despondency and the daily routine was stripped down to coping with the elements. It was the kind of weather that makes old scars ache and throb, the kind of weather that makes life miserable for the soldier, wrote Lt. Dana:

> All is damp and wet and everything feels nasty. It is dismal. The guard is mounted in a cold driving rain, a guard of 200 men. The fatigue and forage parties have gone out to get wet jackets at their work of cutting wood and hay. This kind of weather is the bane of a soldier's life.
>
> The sentinel, wet to the skin, still has to tread his miry post, through mud, and even when relieved has but to sit still for his clothes to dry on him. The ground on which the soldier sleeps is wet, his blanket is wet, his clothes are wet. The rain

extinguishes the fires, and he is obliged to wait until the sun comes out to dry his disagreeable, uncomfortable property. In addition to this, his meals are irregular and half-prepared.

If it rains hard he gets no coffee, so he is obliged to take cold comfort, and if he can get a little whiskey he is apt to raise spirits by artificial means.

With rain sounding on the canvas of his tent, Capt. E. Kirby Smith of the 5th Infantry wrote his wife that he slept in a wet bed for two nights and only kept alive by having a camp kettle of hot coals by my side." Hitchcock noted that some of the officers "constructed small chimneys to their wall tents. I have contented myself with placing a camp kettle with live coals in my tent."

As rain bucketed down and water drizzled through their leaky tents, diarrhea and dysentery plagued the army. The number of cases increased during the winter months, with an average of 10 percent of the officers and 13 percent of the men bedridden. "The whole army . . . might be considered a vast hospital," wrote surgeon John B. Porter. "Hundreds were affected who never entered a sick report."

The miserable days frayed one's temper. The weather was awful, the water brackish, the men sick from dysentery or plain ill-tempered. They were frequently soaked to the bone, slept under wet tents, and woke up cold.

Taylor advised Secretary of War Marcy that they could get by through the winter without having to build huts, that the tents would suffice, though he did order a shipment of lumber from New Orleans to have some of the tents floored.

Sgt. Charles Masland was hospitalized with diarrhea. In a letter home he wrote that, "owing to the very limited means of comfort, the decayed state of the hospital tent, its crowded state, the almost incessant rain and very cold weather, I grew worse daily. I was removed to the general hospital, a building in the town of Corpus Christi.

"I thought I was about to leave this world and become acquainted with the secrets of the great hereafter, see the white robes and hear the harps playing oh so softly."

Not all on the sick list were suffering from bad water and cold weather.

Lt. Isaac Reeve of the 8th Regiment was seriously injured when a horse kicked him near the heart.

Another accident, on Oct. 23, claimed the life of a young second lieutenant, Henry Merrill of the 5th Infantry, who was on board the Augusta in Aransas Bay when he was struck in the head by a falling spar.

The army's cemetery on the bluff, a site selected by Col. Hitchcock after the Dayton explosion, was in use again. Men began to die from dysentery and other causes linked to bad water, poor sanitation, and the cold, rainy weather.

Lt. Col. William Hoffman, commander of the 7th Infantry, died on Nov. 26. He was about 65 and had been ill and infirm at Fort Smith when his regiment was ordered to Corpus Christi, Hitchcock noted that he had been advised not to accompany the regiment "but he insisted upon it, as his regiment was ordered to the field. After he arrived here his chronic diarrhea or dysentery continued and grew worse until he died. A postmortem found that his intestines were in a shocking condition, in some places actually perforated."

Not long after Hoffman was buried, Lt. William T. Allen of the dragoons died.

Taylor's army encampment at Corpus Christi was drawn in October 1845 by Capt. Daniel P. Whiting. Almost half the Army was at Corpus Christi. Courtesy Corpus Christi Central Library.

A wood engraving by an unknown artist shows Corpus Christi in 1845 at the time of the Zachary Taylor encampment. Left, Henry Kinney's home and the tents of the army along the shoreline. Right, village of Corpus Christi.

Corpus Christi

74

Sketch by Seth Eastman shows Corpus Christi after the end of the war. Left, Kinney's home. Right, "Kinney's Tank." Beyond is the village between the bluff and the bay.

Art on preceding pages shown in horizontal perspective.

Gen. Zachary Taylor, 1848, lithograph printed by Francis Michelin. Library of Congress.

Gen. Zachary Taylor, out of uniform, is shown riding his horse in the traditional manner, though he often preferred to ride side-saddle. Taylor was described by one officer as a man who looked like an old farmer with eggs to sell. Sketch by H. R. Robison, from the Library of Congress.

Ethan Allen Hitchcock after 1851 (above) and Daniel P. Whiting. Hitchcock from Library of Congress and Whiting from the Murphy Givens Collection.

Henry Kinney (above) from the Library of Congress and Mauricia Arocha Belden from Murphy Givens Collection.

Lt. U. S. Grant, of the 4ᵗʰ Regiment, at the age of 21, before he arrived with Taylor's army at Corpus Christi. At West Point, fellow cadets called him "Beauty" for his girlish good looks. From the Library of Congress.

Gen. Ulysses S. Grant was elected president after the Civil War. His memoirs, published shortly before his death, devotes considerable attention to his stay at Corpus Christi as a young lieutenant with the 4th Regiment. From the Library of Congress.

Major Gen. George H. Thomas of the Union's Army of the Cumberland, was nicknamed "the Rock of Chickamauga." He was stationed as a young lieutenant at Corpus Christi with the 3rd Artillery in 1845-1846. From "Memoir of Gen. George H. Thomas" by Richard W. Johnson.

Col. David Twiggs, commander of the 2ⁿᵈ Regiment of Dragoons. He was described by a fellow officer as "a hoary headed old lecher." From the Library of Congress.

Gen. William J. Worth, commander of the 8th Infantry, was known as the Marshal Ney of the Army. From the Library of Congress.

Union Gen. John F. Reynolds (above) and Confederate Gen. James Longstreet were both with Zachary Taylor's army at Corpus Christi in the prelude to the Mexican War. Images from the Library of Congress.

*Confederate Gen. Braxton Bragg (top) and Union Gen.
George G. Meade were young lieutenants with Zachary
Taylor's army at Corpus Christi in 1845-1846. Photos
from the Library of Congress.*

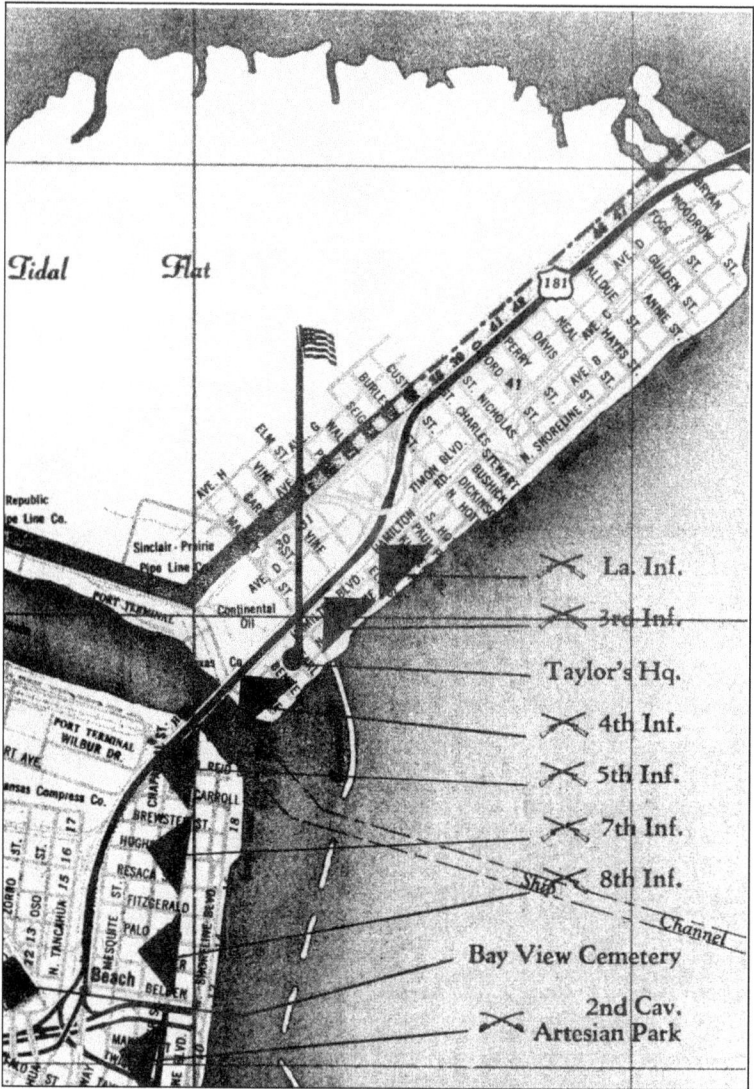

Taylor's encampment at Corpus Christi, from August 1845 to March 1846, shown on an overlay of a 1950-era map of the city. From Joseph Dorst Patch's "The Concentration of General Zachary Taylor's Army at Corpus Christi, Texas."

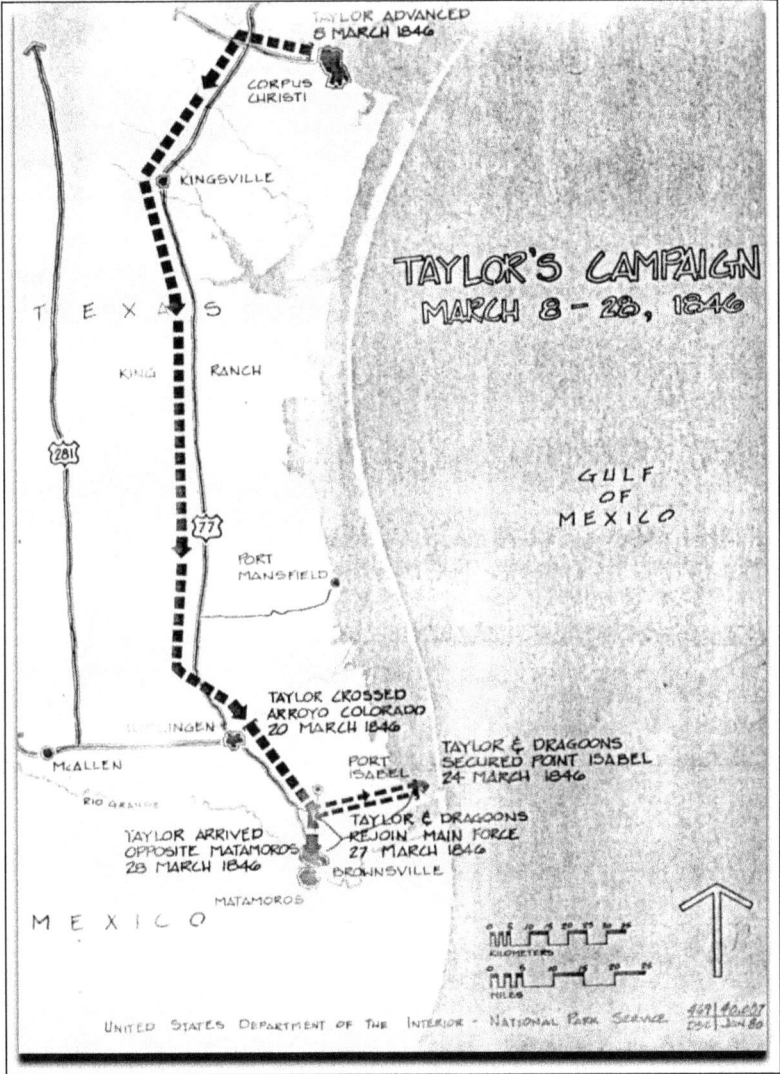

Gen. Zachary Taylor had two routes reconnoitered for the march from Corpus Christi to the Rio Grande across from Matamoros: on Padre Island and down the road taken by Gen. Filisola's army after San Jacinto. He chose the inland route, which ran where U.S. 77 is today

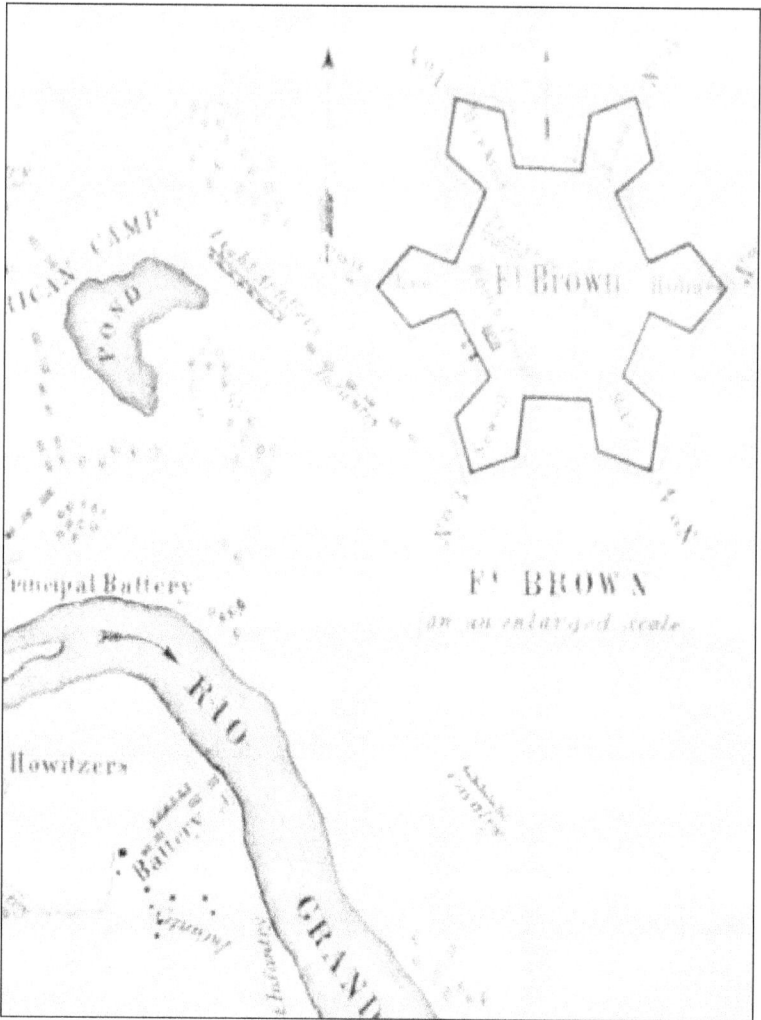

Enlarged detail from a map showing the American fort on the left bank of the Rio Grande, across from the Mexican city of Matamoros. The field work was first called Fort Texas then renamed Fort Brown for Maj. Jacob Brown, a casualty of the bombardment. Map from "A Complete History of the Mexican War" by N. C. Brooks.

Maj. Samuel Ringgold (above) of the 3rd Artillery was one of the heroes of the battle of Palo Alto. Capt. Charles May (below) of the 2nd Dragoons was a hero of the following day's battle at Resaca de la Palma.

Top: Lithograph of the battle of Palo Alto. Published by E.B. and E.C. Kellogg, Hartford, Conn., 1846.

Bottom: Gen. Taylor gives orders at the battle of Resaca de la Palma. Lithograph published by Currier & Ives, New York. Both from the Library of Congress.

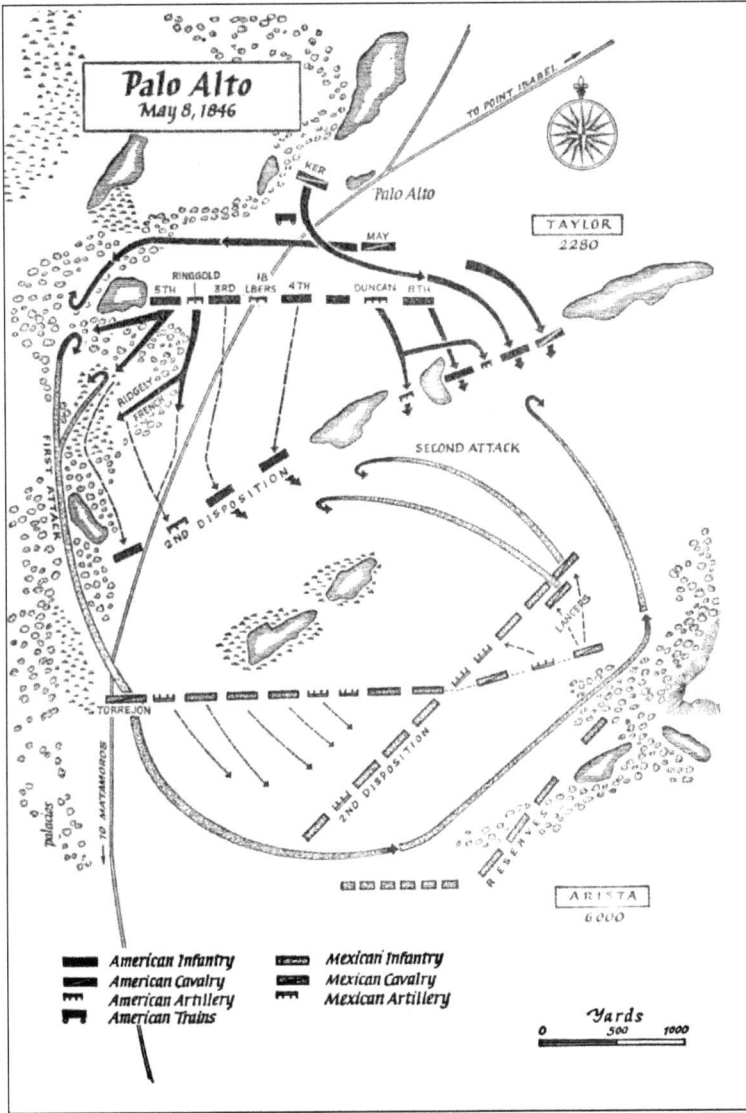

Plan of battle at Palo Alto, the first battle of the Mexican War, fought on May 8, 1846. Art by Rafael Palacios, from "Zach Taylor's Little Army" by Edward J. Nichols.

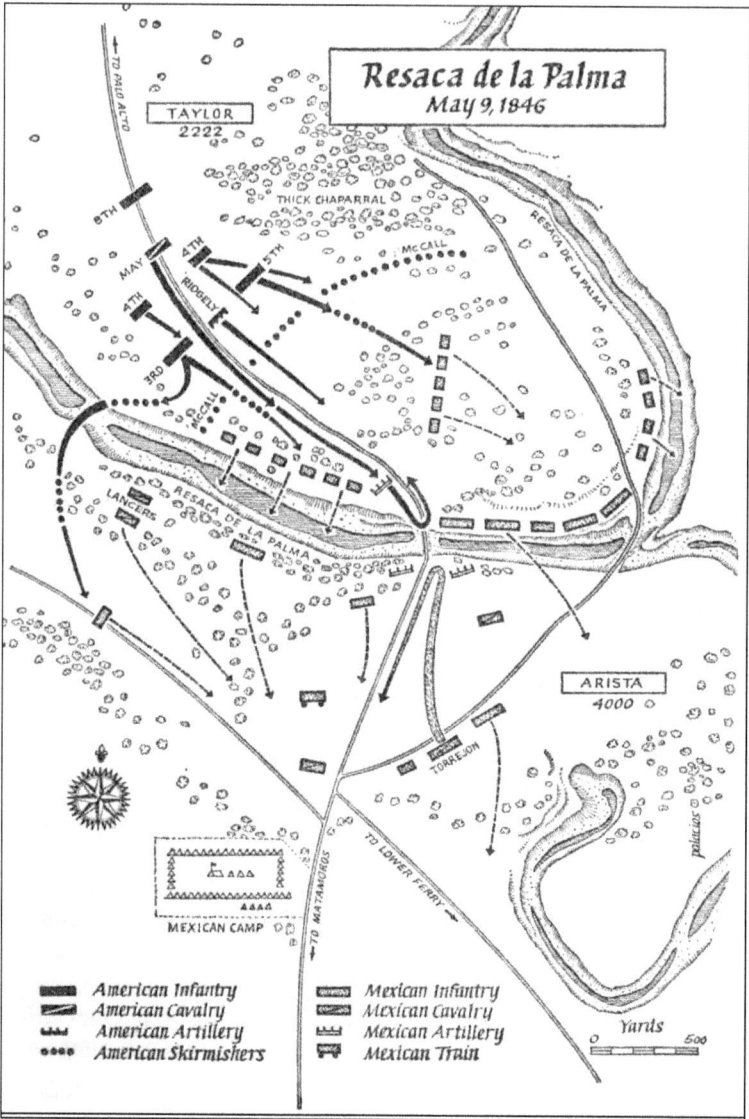

Plan of battle at Resaca de la Palma, fought the day after the battle of Palo Alto. Art by Rafael Palacios, from "Zach Taylor's Little Army" by Edward J. Nichols.

94

A granite slab notes that Zachary Taylor's Army was concentrated in Corpus Christi in 1845-1846. Near where the monument stands, Taylor's soldiers dug an artesian well in what is now Artesian Park.

CHAPTER 10

A Bone-Chilling Norther

At the end of November 1845, Lt. George Gordon Meade of the Topographical Engineers returned from a 10-day exploratory trip down Padre Island and the Laguna Madre to the Rio Grande. He was sent to determine whether Taylor could march his men down the island and send supplies and artillery by boat down the Laguna Madre.

Lt. Meade found that the extreme shallowness, in places, of the laguna would definitely limit the size of the boats that could travel down it. "The supply of wood on the mainland is very limited," he wrote in his report, "no driftwood is to be obtained on the shores and the only supply consists in a few (motts) of live oak which are found two miles back from the shore."

He said the beach on the island formed a natural roadway for 90 miles, uninterrupted by lagoon or bayou. The rest of the island, he said, was not suited for troop movements. Single horsemen, he wrote, could travel down the center of the island, between the dunes, but not large bodies of troops.

After he had written his report, in a letter to his wife, he said the exploring party, under his command, "had very bad weather on the expedition and I was much exposed. On two separate occasions my tent was blown over my head, and I got wet through and through. Indeed, I returned much the worse for my exposure, having become quite bilious and slightly jaundiced."

Conditions were no better at Corpus Christi. If November was wet, and it was, December was very cold.

After Lt. Meade returned from the trip, the weather turned cold "and the high winds that constantly prevail here prevent you from getting your tent comfortable. Indeed, in all my experience of field service, I have never been so comfortless as now. I feel the cold here more than in Maine, because there we had no wind, and plenty of fuel, and could encamp in the woods. Here it is all open beach, where the wind sweeps in gales, day and night, and there is barely wood sufficient for cooking purposes. I shall consider myself lucky if I can get out of it without rheumatism or some such pleasant remembrance of it."

The army learned the meaning of a Texas norther which, one writer wrote later, blows the world inside out and freezes the lining. During late November and early December, wrote Lt. W. S. Henry:

We had the most shocking weather imaginable; either bone-chilling northers or drenching rains, without intermission. Hast thou, dear reader, ever felt a norther or heard tell of one? Well, your northern cold front is nothing to it. The Texas norther comes like a thief in the night and all but steals your life. You go to bed, weather sultry and warm, bed-clothes disagreeable, tent open; before morning you hear a distant rumbling; the roaring increases — the norther comes. For several minutes you hear it careering in its wild course; when it reaches you, it issues fresh from the snow-mountains and with a severity which threatens to prostrate the camp. The change in one's feelings is like an instantaneous transit from the torrid to the frigid zone; blankets are in demand, and no one thinks of living without a good supply on hand. Ice has formed in pails several times, and one morning every tent had an ice covering; the sleet had frozen upon it, and the crackling of the canvas sounded like anything but music. We were forced to throw up embankments and place chaparral to the north of our tents, to break the wind. The men, of course, suffer a great deal. The constant dampness and bad water have produced many serious cases of dysentery. The beauty of this climate is decidedly in the summer. I'll venture to say there is no part of the United States cursed with such a variable one in the winter.

The temperature during the norther dropped to 23 degrees, the coldest weather in the living memory of any of the town's oldest residents, wrote N. S. Jarvis. Ice was half-inch thick on the Nueces River and fish in the bay — pompano, redfish, red snapper, speckled trout and green turtles — were stunned by the cold and gathered along the shore by the cart-load. The supply of fish fed the army for more than a week.

The bitter cold forced Lt. John F. Reynolds, of the 3rd Artillery, to give up sleeping on the ground and move into a bunk. He grumbled about the lack of wood. There were sticks "only for cooking and they are so crooked they won't lie still when you put them down." Smoke rose from the tents through makeshift smokestacks. Capt. George McCall of the 4th had his orderly pour boiling water on his tent flaps, which were frozen solid, to let him out. In a letter home, McCall explained that the winter climate was mild and would be delightful, were it not for the northers which sweep down now and then:

A sad instance, we are told by the people of Corpus Christi, occurred last year in this neighborhood. The wife of a man living a short distance from the town went out on a fine mild morning to drive up her cow. She remained longer than usual and meantime a fierce norther came with terrific violence. As soon as the husband discovered that his wife had not returned, he hurried out in search of her and after searching far and near, at last found, not 200 yards from his own door, the poor wife, who was cold and lifeless. The morning being quite warm, she had gone out lightly clad and the norther had overtaken her at a distance from her home. Before she reached it, the vital principle had been sapped and she fell to the ground to rise no more. This I believe is a well-known fact.

At the encampment, the different regiments surrounded their camps with chaparral bushes to provide extra shelter from the frigid wind. The men were miserable. Their tents were thin, their fires went out, they wanted to be warm.

Col. Hitchcock contented himself with placing a coal scuttle in his tent, filled with live coats, and read Swedenborg, Spinoza and Plato until his head ached, or would have ached if he had been anyone other than Hitchcock.

Lt. R. E. Cochrane of the 4th Regiment had written his parents glowing accounts of Texas when he arrived in August, but after the norther hit he came down with chills and fever and wrote them that "Uncle Sam made a mighty poor bargain when he got Texas, even though he did get it for nothing."

The miseries of the cold and wet weather were compounded by the lack of available firewood. The quartermaster would issue only enough wood for cooking purposes, not for campfires, said a letter from an officer printed in the "Niles National Register."

The men, when not on duty, sat shivering with cold in their wet tents. During the time of cold rains and cutting winds, one of the drummer boys named Tatnall drank too much liquor and under the influence was apt to play practical jokes. A corporal in the 4th Infantry, C. M. Reeves, told the story of one such prank:

A little after dark, Gen. Taylor was sitting in his tent when the drummer boy Tatnall came along, unperceived by any of the officers, and being on a spree and bent on mischief he took out his knife and rip, rip, went the cords of the general's tent. Before the general had time to escape, down it went burying him in its folds. Tatnall ran away at full speed.

As Taylor's orderly was absent, when the general had crawled out, he came over to Col. Garland's tent, where I was stationed as orderly, and got me to go with a detail of men and put things to rights. This being done, he asked me if I knew anything of the fellow who did it.

I had seen the whole transaction. When Tatnall ran he passed so near me that I recognized him. Not wishing to expose him, though, I evaded the question. "General, I did see someone run, but the night is so dark that it was almost impossible to distinguish a man."

The general said, "Well, if I knew who the scoundrel was, I would pull his ears sorely." And this was all that was said about it by that easy tempered old gentleman.

In December, several officers received permission to accompany the paymaster, Maj. Roger S. Dix and his cavalry escort, on a trip to San Antonio. The expedition consisted of 25 men to convoy a wagon train.

Lt. Ulysses S. Grant, among the party, wrote that they saw no inhabitants after Corpus Christi until about 30 miles outside San Antonio. Grant and the other officers stayed in San Antonio while Dix and his escort went on to Austin. When their leave was almost expired, and Dix hadn't returned, Grant and two officers decided to return to Corpus Christi to avoid being listed as absent without leave. They slept on the prairie except for one night at Goliad.

Grant wrote that on the evening of the first day out from Goliad "we heard the most unearthly howling of wolves, directly in our front. The prairie grass was tall, and we could not see the beasts, but the sound indicated they were near. To my ear it appeared that there must have been enough of them to devour our party, horses and all, at a single meal. Lt. Benjamin said, 'Grant, how many wolves do think there are in that pack?' I said, 'Oh, about 20.' In a minute we were in close upon them, before they saw us. There were just two of them. Seated upon their haunches, with their mouths close together, they made all the noise we had been hearing for the past 10 minutes. I have often thought of this incident when I have heard the noise of a few disappointed politicians who have deserted their associates. There are always more of them before they are counted."

A more serious incident than Grant's pack of two wolves happened on the paymaster's trip at San Antonio, described by Lt. Samuel G. French:

When I learned that a train of paymaster wagons would leave for San Antonio, I got a month's leave to accompany it, along with W. L.

Crittenden and some others. At San Patricio the Nueces River was too high and the wagons couldn't cross. Crittenden and I and two men from Kentucky cut loose from the train and proceeded on the journey. Our guide was a Mr. Campbell, who lived in San Antonio. We reached San Antonio in four days. Lands were offered us at six cents per acre that commands now over a thousand dollars per acre, and the population is at present fifty thousand.

My stay in San Antonio depended on the departure of the train. There were a number of army officers waiting the convenience and protection of the wagons. Most of the officers had arrived at the camping ground in advance of the wagons and were sitting under the trees.

As the train was passing by, Crittenden took from his pocket what was called a pepper-box pistol and fired at a tree parallel to the road. Lt. Lafayette McLaws (of the 7th Infantry) left the train and shouted "Quit firing, I am shot!"

As he was not in range, no one regarded what he said and Crittenden kept on firing the revolver. When McLaws rode up he had a wild look and the bosom of his shirt was red with blood. A ball that hit the tree had glanced off at an angle and struck him in the chest.

He was taken from his horse and put in a wagon to be taken back to San Antonio. The wound was probed by a surgeon and the ball discovered near the spine. He soon recovered and came back to Corpus Christi.

The theater that was being built in November, which W. S. Henry said was of no inconsiderable dimensions, opened on Dec. 11. It was the Union Theater, the first of two built to provide an entertainment venue for the soldiers. The other, the Army Theater, was built under the supervision of army officers led by John B. Magruder and James Longstreet; it opened a month later.

The Union Theater was designed and built by Charles G. Bryant, an architect from Bangor, Maine. Like so many of the citizens of Corpus Christi, Bryant was a wanted man elsewhere. He had been involved in a rebellion in Canada and when it failed, he was posted as wanted in Canada for sedition and in Maine for violating the neutrality act. In 1839, he arrived in Galveston then moved on to Corpus Christi in 1845, where he built the Union Theater. It was a large building that could seat hundreds. When it opened, admission prices were $1 for a box seat and 50 cents for the pit. In front of the theater, and connected to it, was a large saloon that advertised "the choicest liquors, wines, fruits and segars."

A long-simmering quarrel over brevet rank erupted in December. This was an old dispute in the army. Brevet rank was intended to reward officers for their actions in battle or for other outstanding achievements. A mandated limit on the number of officers, from second lieutenant to major general, blocked younger officers from promotion until senior officers died or retired. A brevet was an honorary promotion that did not include the equivalent pay.

The dispute was over whether a brevet promotion outranked someone senior in the line. Several events brought this issue to the forefront at Corpus Christi, with the focus on Worth and Twiggs.

Brevet Brig. Gen. William J. Worth loved the gold buttons and feathered plumes of a fancy uniform, like Gen. Winfield Scott. Because of his reputation as a fighting man, he was called the Marshal Ney* of the army but he was a

---

* Worth was sometimes called him "Old Stampede" because in a temper he would rush off in every direction at the same time.

cross-grained man who would resign, or threaten to resign, at the slightest provocation. Col. David E. Twiggs of the dragoons, with a bull neck and bull voice, was beloved by his soldiers for his profanity, drinking and womanizing. Hitchcock called him "a hoary-headed old lecher."

Worth and Twiggs began to squabble over seniority. Both Worth and Twiggs had fiery tempers, were heavy drinkers and didn't like each other. When Worth asserted that he was senior in rank based upon his brevet promotion, Twiggs bristled with anger. Worth did hold a higher brevet rank but Twiggs was senior in the line of command.

The brevet quarrel became more than academic when rumors swept the camp that Gen. Taylor was considering retirement. If he did retire, his successor would likely be one of the two most senior officers, Gen. Worth or Col. Twiggs.

The issue surfaced when a lieutenant colonel, who had brevet rank, directed some lieutenants who had brevets to assume command on the parade ground over their own captains. Lt. Abner Doubleday wrote that the captains sheathed their swords and walked away. "As it was evident that enforcement of the order would create a mutiny, the matter was referred to the authorities in Washington for decision. There, Gen. Winfield Scott stood up strongly for brevet rank, but the secretary of war held the contrary view."

Since most officers did not hold brevet rank, there was strong opposition to Scott's position. Gen. Taylor was on the brevet side, therefore Worth's side, though he told an adjutant that Worth had been "pampered and bloated with ego for things he never done." Hitchcock and most of the officers were on Twiggs' side, that of seniority in line.

"The jealousies of army life continued to annoy," wrote Hitchcock. "Shortly afterwards, Taylor ordered a review, designating Twiggs to command and Worth made such a violent protest that Taylor dispensed with the review."

A letter of protest (which was called a "memorial") was drawn up by Col. Hitchcock and signed by 158 officers, from Col. Twiggs and Col. Whistler down to the second lieutenants. The letter noted that the subject had been a controversy in the army since the War of 1812 and argued that giving precedence to brevet rank would violate law and reason. It appealed to the Senate to override Scott, the general of the army, and set the matter right.

FOUR DAYS before Christmas, Hitchcock dreamed of his brother Henry, who had been dead six years, and his deceased mother, Lucy Allen Hitchcock. In the dream, they were sitting at a dinner table which was silent like a church show, and his brother Henry took his (Ethan's) knife and cut some of the meat on the table. Hitchcock himself couldn't share in the meal because Henry had taken his knife.[*] "My faculties were aroused and I waked and found myself in camp bed at Corpus Christi, where the real is very vivid and not to be mistaken for the ideal. I thought the dream a singular one and intended to notice it here. I had this strange dream some five or six nights since."

---

[*] Hitchcock's brother Henry was Chief Justice of the Alabama Supreme Court when he died of yellow fever on Aug. 11, 1839. Hitchcock's mother, Lucy Caroline Allen Hitchcock, died in Burlington, Vt., on Aug. 27, 1842.

CHAPTER 11

"Be Sure You Are Right"

New Year's Day 1846 was mild and balmy, almost like high summer, not like winter at all. Col. Ethan Allen Hitchcock, commander of the 3rd Infantry Regiment, was getting dressed when he remembered that it was the first morning of the New Year and noted in his diary, with haughty disapproval, that the day would go as other days with drinking, horse-racing, gambling, and theatrical amusements.

Howes & Maybie Circus had arrived from New Orleans to entertain the troops and a ball was set for the evening, but the Spinoza-reading Hitchcock, the scholar of mystic philosophy, said he would take no part in the day's amusements but would take refuge in his tent.

Gen. Taylor celebrated the convivial spirit of the day by inviting officers to share a glass of eggnog at his headquarters' tent.* Lt. George Gordon Meade wrote his wife that he had spent a rather stupid day for the first day of the year. "In the morning I was engaged in making official

---

* Capt. George A. McCall of the 4th Infantry said his tent was not more than 25 yards from the beach, past an inlet to the bay. Near him was Gen. Taylor's headquarters' tent, said McCall, on a slight elevation 15 feet from the beach. Taylor's headquarters was just north of what later was called Hall's Bayou in the proximity of today's Texas State Aquarium.

complimentary visits to the 'big-bugs' of the camp, all of whom had eggnog and cake for their visitors; then we had a race, gotten up by the officers for their amusement; then I dined with a party who endeavored to be as merry as they could under the circumstances; and, in the evening, I accompanied them to the theater; for you must know that since our arrival here they have built a theater and imported a company of strolling actors, who murder tragedy, burlesque comedy, and render farce into buffoonery, in the most approved style.

New Year's Day marked the publication of the first issue of Corpus Christi's first newspaper, the "Gazette," which was said to be "the most western journal in the English language on the American continent." It was published by pioneer Texas printer Samuel Bangs, who came over from Galveston, and his partner in the enterprise, George W. Fletcher, a Corpus Christi physician. The editor was an influential member of the community, Jose de Alba.

The "Gazette" featured new type and woodcuts, included a section printed in Spanish, and cost 10 cents a copy or $5 for a year's subscription. The slogan under the masthead of the "Gazette" was adopted from David Crockett's motto, "Be Sure You Are Right, Then Go Ahead."

Col. Hitchcock noted in his diary that, "We now have a newspaper at this place" and in New Orleans "The Daily Picayune" announced its arrival: "A new and spirited paper just started (in Corpus Christi) by Bangs and Fletcher." In Baltimore the "Niles National Register" later wrote, "We see there is a 'Corpus Christi Gazette' now quoted by the Washington papers. It is to be hoped we shall have regular bulletins from our gallant little army."

Bangs, who bought his press in Galveston, did well, judging by the paid advertisements, wrote Edward J. Nichols in "Zach Taylor's Little Army." Some of the ads in that first edition included:

—F. Gonzales was offering 40 boxes of claret of very special brand — St. Julien Medoc.

—F. Helmuller announced 40 boxes of chewing tobacco — Hong's, Clark's, Henry's, Robinson's, Moore's, and A. Cabanes's.

—D. Wolf & Company would faithfully attend customers desiring dry goods, clothing, and liquor.

—John P. Kelsey would thankfully receive all orders for horses, mules, and breeding mares and fill them at the lowest rates.

—William Mann & Company had on hand 50 barrels of whiskey, 20 of cider, 15 boxes of lemons; also port, claret, and sherry.

—Conrad Meuly had coffee and hot drinks, bread, and pastry of every variety constantly on hand.

—J. R. Mills could supply beef, pork, mutton, and venison; also could supply steamboat (passages) and shipping at the shortest notice.

Nichols said such notices in the "Gazette" made it read as if Corpus Christi was a going town even without adding the "Great Western Eating Salon," the "Stop That Ball!" bowling alleys, Capt. Kilgore's Tin-Pin Alley and Oyster Parlor, or "All the Comforts of Home" in the Kinney House.

Lt. John Reynolds sent his family in Lancaster, Pa., a copy of the "Gazette." "You must not imagine from this paper," he warned, "that we have all the luxuries and amusements it would lead you to suppose upon a mere perusal of the advertisements." Reynolds added a new list of items on sale — carved furniture, music boxes, jewelry, and notions. It was nothing but junk stacked in a row of canvas sheds. He wrote off the eating houses and grog shops as vile. "Corpus, he said, was one of the rowdiest, cutthroat places he had ever seen."

One edition of the "Gazette" printed the names of all the officers in Taylor's "Army of Occupation" at Corpus Christi and another reported on the arrival of trading parties from the border and the loss of the schooner Victoria, loaded with government stores, which wrecked off the Aransas Bar. The "Gazette" was published from Jan. 1, 1846 to April 2, 1846, after the army had departed for the Rio Grande.

The first edition of the "Gazette" reported that Charles Bryant's Union Theater, which was built in November and opened on Dec. 11, would stage performances of "La Polka" and "The Ambassador's Ball." On Jan. 8 the town's second theater, the Army Theater, opened with a play called "The Wife — A Tale of Mantua" by James Sheridan Knowles.

The Army Theater was constructed under the supervision of army officers led by Capt. John B. Magruder of the 1st Artillery and Lt. James Longstreet of the 8th. W. S. Henry described the Army Theater as "a capital building, capable of seating some 800 persons. The scenes were painted by officers of the army. A very clever company was engaged and many an otherwise dreary evening was spent by many of us with infinite pleasure within its walls."

Lt. James Longstreet in his memoirs wrote:

> The officers built a theater, depending upon their own efforts to reimburse them. As there was no one outside the army except two rancheros within 100 miles, our dramatic company was organized from among the officers, who took both male and female characters. In farce and comedy we did well enough, and soon collected funds to pay for the building and incidental expenses.
>
> The house was filled every night. Gen. Worth always encouraged us, Gen. Taylor sometimes, and Gen. Twiggs occasionally. We found

ourselves in funds sufficient to send over to New Orleans for costumes and concluded to try tragedy. The 'Moor of Venice' was chosen. Lt. Theodoric Porter was selected to be the Moor Othello and Lt. U. S. Grant[*] was to play Desdemona, the daughter of Brabantio. After rehearsal, Porter protested that a male heroine (Grant) could not support the character or give sentiment to the part (Porter had some difficulty trying to kiss Grant). We sent to New Orleans and secured Mrs. Hart to play the role of Desdemona. Then all went well.

ON THE DAY THE ARMY THEATER opened, a duel was fought between Lt. Edward Deas of the 4th Artillery and a sutler (army storekeeper) named Irwin. The two men met on the field of honor, exchanged shots to no effect, shook hands and agreed that the affair was "honorably terminated."

Col. Hitchcock noted that the duel came about over a gambling matter between two other officers. A few days earlier, Lt. Randolph Ridgely of 3rd Artillery and Maj. W. W. Morris of the 4th Artillery were playing brag (the card game Lt. Grant swore off of at Jesup) for high stakes at Erwin's sutler's store and Ridgely lost a large sum of money.

Later, at a mess table, Lt. Deas said he thought Maj. Morris had taken advantage of Ridgely while the lieutenant was too drunk to know what he was doing. The sutler, Erwin, argued that Lt. Ridgeley was fully capable of managing his own affairs at gaming. This led to harsh words, some blows, a challenge, and the duel that was

---

[*] Grant was nicknamed "Beauty" at West Point for his girlish good looks.

111

"honorably terminated" with missed shots and no bloodshed.

A day or so later Lt. Ridgely sent a draft for $600[*] to Maj. Morris, who sent back a note offering to return it, but Ridgeley, said Hitchcock, refused to hear anything more of the matter.

On Jan. 11, a Sunday, Hitchcock took a walk with Capt. Thomas Cram of the Topographical Engineers. The day was "exceedingly beautiful" and unseasonably warm for January as they walked on the bluff above the camp. Later that day, Hitchcock rode south of town where he came upon a brickyard and two "Negro huts."

From inside of one of the houses he heard the silence broken by a simple Methodist hymn. "I sat on my horse overlooking the calm bay, with the sun shining brightly, and thought what a happiness it would be to live in this world if it were not a place for sin and misery and all sorts of wretchedness." The scholar of mystic philosophy said he rode him in "a pensive mood — a little saddened."

On the evening of Jan. 13, Hitchcock wrote in his diary that the encampment was swept by a violent rain from the southeast, but it was not very cold.

As the sun came out next morning, Hitchcock stayed in his tent reading "a very remarkable book" by a German mystic philosopher, Henry Cornelius Agrippa, "The Vanity of Arts and Sciences." Hitchcock said Agrippa "abuses the Roman Church without mercy" and showed the book to an army surgeon, Dr. Alfred W. Kennedy, "who, though much amused, thought Agrippa a disappointed misanthropic man."

On Jan. 21, Lt. George Gordon Meade wrote his wife that he was leaving on an expedition, under the command of Capt. Joseph Mansfield, to examine Aransas Bay. Their first stop was at the depot on St. Joseph's Island, 30 miles

---

[*] Today's dollar equivalent would amount to $20,000.

from Corpus Christi. The expedition was planned to visit the towns of Copano, Lamar, La Baca (Lavaca), Linnville, and Matagorda. Meade said they were prepared and fitted out for a month's expedition. He later wrote from Matagorda:

My last letter to you was of the date of the 26th (January) written at St. Joseph's, just on the eve of my departure. Since then we have been knocking about the bays between Corpus Christi and this place, making surveys, and visiting towns and places where towns are to be. Our expedition has been more agreeable than I anticipated, although we have had as bad weather as we could have anticipated.

I have never experienced more hospitality than has been extended to us by the inhabitants wherever they have had it in their power, and at Matagorda we are quite in clover. This little town has about 500 people, but they are of a much better class than those you generally meet with, as it is one of the old settlements of the country, and has a great deal of substantial wealth in it.

I have, besides, met several people here from Philadelphia, and have been much gratified at being able to talk of the old place. Among other people here I found a Dr. Hultner, an excellent musician, especially on the harp, who resided some time in Philadelphia, and had given lessons to many of our acquaintances, and to whom I was drawn from the simple fact of his telling me he had often heard you play."

CHAPTER 12

Dancing at the Annexation Ball

In the first week of February, Col. Ethan Allen Hitchcock wrote in his diary that Gen. Taylor received orders "to move to the Rio Grande and he has declared his purpose of going to the north bank directly opposite to Matamoros. This will make a considerable stir."

Hitchcock, always quick to predict a gloomy outcome, wrote that, "For my own part I see no object in it but to expose the troops to disease by being on the river bank instead of being on the seashore."

Hitchcock believed Taylor would deviate from what he thought was right — even what he *knew* was right — if it would serve his ambition. As Hitchcock had written when they first arrived at Corpus Christi — *If he succeeds, it will be by accident.*

As to the right of the planned movement to the Rio Grande, Hitchcock wrote, "I have said from the first that the United States are the aggressors. We have outraged the Mexican government and people by an arrogance and presumption that deserve to be punished. For ten years we have been encroaching on Mexico and insulting her.

"The Mexicans have in the whole of this time done but two wrong things: one was the destruction of the Constitution of 1824, which would have converted Texas into a mere department of Mexico; this gave Texas the right of revolution and she established her independence as far west as the Nueces; the other was the cold-blooded and

115

savage murder of James Fannin's men at Goliad — an individual piece of barbarity which has deprived the Mexican army of all respect among civilized people. Beyond these, I know of nothing Mexico has done to deserve censure." Hitchcock, in a melancholic mood, also noted:

> My heart is not in the business. I am against it from the bottom of my soul as a most unholy and unrighteous proceeding. It looks as if the government sent a small force on purpose to bring on a war, so as to have a pretext for taking California and as much of the country as possible. Whatever becomes of this army, there is no doubt of a war between the United States and Mexico.
>
> I fear I am not in my proper vocation — that is, I have read and studied myself out of it. The study of philosophy and my general reading have subdued all spirit for action and induced a wish to retire from the world into some solitude.

Lt. W. S. Henry had no doubts about whether the move south was correct. "It is idle to discuss the propriety of the move. In annexing Texas, we were bound to take her as she was, with her prescribed limits, which she claimed to be the Rio Grande."

On Feb. 8, Rev. John Hayne, a Methodist minister, preached a sermon at the Union Theater. The congregation consisted mainly of officers and soldiers of the army.

Hitchcock wrote on Feb. 14 that "a boisterous cold norther passed over us yesterday. But today we have fine weather." He noted that he had been reading Mary Shelley's "Rambles in Germany and Italy," but could find no evidence of her talent.

On Feb. 16 an "Annexation Ball" was held at the Union Theater to mark the official end of the Republic of Texas and the emergence of the state.* The invitation read:

ANNEXATION BALL

The company of Mrs. Belden is respectfully solicited at a ball to be given by the officers of the United States army and citizens of Corpus Christi at the Union Theater on Monday evening, Feb. 16, 1846.

The Managers

Music at the ball was provided by five army bands and among the tunes played was one created for the occasion called "General Taylor's Encampment Quick Step." The town's leading citizens and army officers attended the ball. Sponsors included Charles Bryant, J. P. Kelsey, William Mann, William Aubrey, and Jose de Alba. (Many years later, Mrs. Mollie Woessner would relate the story that her aunt, Ellen Pettigrew, "led the grand march with Gen. Taylor in Corpus Christi at the Annexation Ball. Aunt Ellen once showed me the dress she wore. It was of dotted swiss, hand-embroidered by herself, with a wide full skirt and a tight waist, and drop shoulders. Gen. Taylor picked her out for his partner because she was the prettiest girl in Corpus Christi.")

With Taylor's orders to move the army to the Rio Grande, a new current of energy surged throughout the encampment. It was all hugger-mugger, hurry and suppressed excitement in preparations for the departure.

---

* At a ceremony in Austin, the Lone Star Flag was lowered and replaced by the Stars and Stripes. J. Pinckney Henderson was sworn in as the first governor and President Anson Jones declared, "The final act in this great drama is now performed. The Republic of Texas is no more."

Time had passed wearily during the winter months, wrote Cpl. C. M. Reeves of the 4th Infantry. "It was hard duty and plenty of it. A soldier must take things patiently and, like a machine, cannot move except at the bidding of a master hand. We were glad when the order came to break up and march to the Rio Grande."

There was a great business in finding and buying the means of transportation. The quartermasters for some weeks had been scouring the area buying horses, mules, oxen, and wagons and carts to carry the army's supplies and equipment. Lt. W. S. Henry of the 3rd Infantry wrote that "the most active means were used by the quartermaster's department to collect transportation. We were miserably deficient; wild mules were purchased and broken; and everything, you may say, had to be created out of nothing."

German colonists bound for New Braunfels and the Hill Country were stranded at Indian Point (later Indianola) for lack of wagons and ox-carts to move their goods inland. All the freighters' rolling stock was hired by the government and sent on the roads to Corpus Christi. One activity in preparation for the move, wrote Lt. U. S. Grant, "consisted of securing mules and getting them broken to harness. The animals sold to the government were all young and unbroken, even to the saddle, and were quite as wild as the wild horses of the prairie." Grant wrote that the wild mules and horses were driven into a corral and:

> The Mexicans, who were all experienced in throwing the lasso, would go into the corral on horseback with their lassos attached to the pommels of their saddles. Soldiers detailed as teamsters and blacksmiths would also enter the corral, the former with ropes to serve as halters, and the latter with branding irons and a fire to keep the irons heated.

A lasso was thrown over the neck of a mule, when he would rush to the length of the tether, first one end then the other. While he was plunging and gyrating, another lasso would be thrown, catching the animal by a forefoot. This would bring the mule to the ground. Then he was seized and held by the teamsters while the blacksmith impressed upon him with hot irons, "U.S." The delivery of that mule was then complete. The same process was gone through with every mule and wild horse with the army of occupation.

Grant's company commander,. Capt. George A. McCall, in a letter to his brother, said the chief quartermaster reported to Gen. Taylor that the quartermaster at New Orleans had sent the number of wagons that had been requested but five of them would be without teams, as the number of mules sent was 25 less than the number required.

"This brought from the general one of his choleric expressions against the Quartermaster's Department, of which he is no great admirer," McCall wrote. The general suddenly was all business. "With his usual quickness of decision, he directed the officer to send him all the Mexicans in camp. The General, when they were assembled in front of his tent, told them he wanted 50 wild horses, for which they would be paid a fair price.

"In half an hour, four of these men were mounted and off for the plains, where the mustangs collect in vast numbers. Here they built from the nearest mesquite woods a corral with a funnel entrance, into which they forced some 70 wild horses and in ten days from the time they started drove into the quartermaster's corral here, upwards of 50 of them. Twenty-five of the best were soon selected, lassoed, thrown, haltered, and delivered into the hands of the teamsters who had been selected to break them into harness.

"The docility of these horses is astonishing. The teamsters, old horsemen, after a couple of days, induced them to eat a little grass, cut for them; then they buckled a collar upon their necks, and so on with the rest of the harness, when they suffered themselves in a few days to be led about the corral. Finally, five (all bays) were attached to each wagon, and with a man at the head of each horse, started, in train, to make a circuit in front of the camp.

"This was accomplished without the slightest accident. The teamsters have taught them to eat hay and corn; they also begin to put a log or two, or some other light weight, into the wagon, and as they are exercised for two or three hours twice a day, it is not doubted that they will be ready for the march by the early part of next month, when the general plans advancing to the Rio Grande. The rest of the horses were speedily disposed of by the Mexicans to officers and others in camp. I bought a beautiful young mare, an iron-gray, for five dollars. In a few days she suffered herself to be mounted and ridden slowly about without opposition."

AS THE MONTH OF FEBRUARY entered its last week, all was hustle, bustle and excitement. Lt. John James Peck wrote, "We are preparing as fast as possible and only want the result of the exploring parties to start." Before any movement began, Taylor first had to determine the fitness of the terrain for the passage of a marching army with an immense baggage train, the availability of water and grass for the horses, and which route to the south offered the best conditions.

Taylor had sent out two patrols to look for a suitable route of march. One party under Capt. W. J. Hardee of the 2nd Dragoons traveled down the middle of Padre Island. Another scouting party under Capt. William M. Graham of the 4th Regiment followed the same route the defeated Mexican Army used 10 years before after its defeat at San Jacinto.

The recon parties returned on Feb. 21. Surgeon N. S. Jarvis wrote in his journal: "Capt. Graham and his party returned from the expedition towards the Rio Grande by the Matamoros Road. They proceeded about 100 miles on that route, encountered no obstacles, and describe the road for most of the distance as good with a sufficiency of water and grass."

The other detachment under Capt. Hardee, which explored the island route, returned at about the same time. "They proceeded as far as Brazos Santiago at the foot of the island and describe the road the whole distance along the seashore as delightful, being perfectly smooth and hard and nearly in a straight line. They saw numbers of wild game and cattle on the lower part of the island. On their march down they came across several skeletons that marked the spot where an encounter took place between some Mexicans and (Karankawa) Indians two or three years since."

Because of a shortage of forage for horses and draft animals, Taylor chose the route explored by Capt. Graham's party, the old Spanish trading route south. Taylor limited each company to 1,500 pounds of luggage and directed each infantryman and dragoon to carry 100 cartridges. Artillery companies were ordered to carry 100 rounds for each gun. Two mules and a wagon were chosen to haul Gen. Taylor's personal possessions.

The prospect of the army's immediate departure found no favor with the merchants of the town, wrote Lt. George Gordon Meade, who stood in fear of losing their livelihoods.

"The good people of Corpus Christi," wrote Meade, "who have been living on us as did the flies on the fox in the fable, and who see in our departure the total breaking up of their place, have been making the most gigantic efforts to frighten the general from going, on the plea of there being a very large Mexican force ready to oppose him; but Gen. Taylor is not to be turned in this way from a matter of duty, and he told them if there were fifty thousand Mexicans he would try his best to get there."

Packing up was the order of the day. Sgt. Charles Masland of the 3rd wrote that, "Here and there might be seen groups of Mexicans bargaining with our men for wearing apparel and giving cash for what they might have had for nothing in a few days, for we could not carry half our plunder."

The soldiers were happy to be going somewhere, anywhere, for the novelty, if nothing else. As the New York Journal wrote in the spring of 1845 when the prospect of war with Mexico was the topic of the day — *Well, there would be fun in that. Some interest, something to talk about.* They were soldiers, fighters to a man, and ready for a scrap.

Lt. Henry was delighted at the prospects of the march. "We have become restless and anxious for a change; we anticipate no little fun, and all sorts of adventure, upon the route."

On March 4, Capt. William M. Graham and 100 men of the 4th Regiment left with 60 wagons filled with supplies to establish a depot on Santa Gertrudis Creek, 40 miles from Corpus Christi, about one-third of the way to the Rio Grande.

As the troops prepared to leave Corpus Christi, Gen. Taylor in a dispatch to Secretary of War Marcy wrote, "The roads are in good order, the weather fine, and the troops in excellent condition for service."

On March 6, Lt. Edmund Kirby Smith[*] wrote his mother that the army was preparing to march south:

> We are on the eve of a march to the Mexican frontier and three weeks will see our tents glistening along the banks of the Rio Grande, or our bones whitening on the plains which separate us from that famed river. The prospect of active service has worked a great change in our little host.
>
> All is hustle and excitement. The eyes of the most listless now sparkle with the mention of the Mexicano and our anxiety to move increases. Such sharpening of swords, repairing of firearms, such a demand for revolvers and bowie knives, Corpus Christi never saw.
>
> The dragoons were marched down to the Quartermaster's and were occupied some time in grinding and sharpening their sabers. All betokens a speedy move and a decided expectation of a brush with the Mexicans ere we reach Matamoros.
>
> The order of march has been published. The army will move in four columns with an interval of a day's march between them. The Second Dragoons with Ringgold's Artillery leave day after to-morrow, constituting the first column. Worth's Brigade and Duncan's Company, the second; McIntosh's Brigade, the third; Colonel Whistler's Brigade and a company of artillery, the fourth.
>
> We will leave quite a pleasant station (for Texas) at Corpus Christi, and I feel quite loth to give up the luxuries and comforts we have been so

---

[*] His older brother, also with the army, was Capt. Ephraim Kirby Smith. Both used the name, E. Kirby Smith.

long collecting around us, even for the fandangos and black-eyed senoritas of Matamoros. The climate here is really delightful; nor are we entirely out of the world at Corpus Christi. Two theaters, a morning paper and a line of boats to New Orleans are luxuries not to be despised.

Lt. Meade wrote his wife that "the orders are out. The dragoons and Major Ringgold's company of artillery move on the eighth (Sunday) and the First, Second and Third Brigades follow on each succeeding day. My position is not yet settled, as I thought it was, as it was intimated to me I would probably accompany the dragoons in the advance. This is very agreeable to me, as my proper position is with the advance party. My next letter will be from the banks of the Rio Grande."

CHAPTER 13

Marching Orders

Now it was March and they were going south, to the Rio Grande. In the first days of the month, preparations were completed and the camp was in a state of high excitement. Gen. Taylor issued the army's marching orders, which were published in the "Corpus Christi Gazette".

"The Army of Occupation is about to take up a position on the left bank of the Rio Grande. As the army is marching to the frontier on a delicate service, the commanding general wishes it distinctly understood that no person not properly attached to it will be permitted to accompany the troops or establish themselves in their vicinity, either on the route or on the Rio Grande, on any pretense whatever. It may save individuals useless expense and annoyance to be informed that rigid measures will be taken to enforce this regulation, which is deemed necessary for the interests of public service."

The gamblers, saloon-keepers and camp followers still managed to make their way south and eventually set themselves up on the border in proximity to the troops.

One battery of heavy siege guns, some of General Taylor's headquarters staff, and the convalescent sick were moved by water to the hospital on St. Joseph's Island and to Brazos Santiago at the mouth of the Rio Grande.

The expedition was escorted not by a man-of-war but by

the revenue cutter Woodbury* with Capt. Foster in command. The rest of the army marched south by four columns with one day's interval between them.

Col. David "Old Bull" Twiggs and the 2nd Dragoons with a battery of light artillery left on Sunday, March 8. It was a clear day, but oppressively hot, as they marched away, at 10 in the morning. Army drummers beat out an old rollicking marching-away tune, "The Girl I Left Behind Me" with the lyrics:

> *I seek for one as fair and gay*
> *But find none to remind me*
> *How sweet the hours I passed away*
> *With the girl I left behind me.*

"It certainly is a pretty air and very appropriate when troops are marching," wrote Sgt. Charles Masland, "but our commander rode up and shouted, 'Stop that, sir! Who told you to play that damn song?' "

The next day, Monday, Col. William J. Worth left with the 1st Brigade and Lt. James Duncan's battery. The 1st Brigade included the 8th Infantry and the 4th Artillery.

On Tuesday, March 10, Col. James S. McIntosh, "Old Tosh," started off with the 2nd Brigade, which included the 5th and 7th regiments of infantry.

On Wednesday, March 11, Col. William Whistler's 3rd Brigade, the 3rd artillery, and Taylor's headquarters closed up the rear. The 3rd Brigade included the 3rd and 4th regiments of infantry. Elements of Hitchcock's 3rd Infantry were the first to arrive on Aug. 1, 1845 and were the last to leave. Lt. W. S. Henry looked back at the site where Taylor's army had camped for the past seven months. "The

---

* The Porpoise and the Lawrence, two brigs of war, were already at Point Isabel, where the Rio Grande enters the Gulf, 25 miles from Matamoros, where Taylor planned to establish a supply depot.

fields of white canvas were no longer visible and the campground looked like desolation itself. But the bright waters of the bay looked as sweet as ever."

TAYLOR'S MARCHING ORDERS limited each company to 1,500 pounds of baggage. To carry the supplies, Edward J. Nichols ("Zach Taylor's Little Army") wrote that "a train of 307 ox- and mule-drawn wagons rattled along behind the columns. Some of the heavier wagons were pulled by oxen and others by mules. Altogether an army of 3,354 officers and men were tramping ahead on disputed soil."

One of the ammunition wagons was adapted to carry Col. Ethan Allen Hitchcock of the 3rd Infantry. The mystic philosopher was too sick with his chronic dysentery to ride. Dr. A. W. Kennedy advised him not to travel with the regiment but Hitchcock insisted. On the way to the Rio Grande he rested on a makeshift bed on boxes of ammunition in a wagon pulled by oxen.

Hitchcock wrote in his diary, "I was sick and in bed three days before the 3rd brigade marched and was strongly urged by Doctor Kennedy, Captain Larnard, and my adjutant not to attempt to accompany the regiment. Craig and others urged the same thing. But I knew the importance to myself individually of coming, if possible, and I have come thus far under every disadvantage — riding a number of days in an ox-wagon on a bed laid on boxes of ammunition. The last two or three days I have ridden on my horse but am exceedingly fatigued and weak to the last degree."

Lt. Grant later wondered why it was thought necessary to allow a day's interval between the departure of the four brigades. "In view of the immense bodies of men moved on the same day over narrow roads, through dense forests, and across large streams, in our late war (Civil War), it seems strange now that a body of three thousand men should have been broken into four columns, separated by a day's march."

Perhaps Taylor wasn't concerned about separating the army since intelligence reports confirmed there had been no hostile troops movements by Mexico. He could take his time and separate the army, which would allow for better water and forage on the advance south. He later concentrated the army at the Arroyo Colorado.

INFANTRY OFFICERS WHO HAD who had their own horses were allowed to ride, but Grant, who had purchased four mustangs at Corpus Christi, had lost his when his servant let them escape when he was taking them to water. Grant said his company commander, Capt. George A. McCall of the 4th Infantry, had two good horses, one for himself and one for his servant.

"He (McCall) was quite anxious to know whether I did not intend to get me another horse before the march began. I told him no. I belonged to a foot regiment. I did not understand the object of his solicitude at the time, but when we were about to start, he said, 'Grant, there is a horse for you.' I found that he could not bear the idea of his servant riding on a long march while his lieutenant went afoot. He had found a mustang — a three-year-old colt only recently captured — which had been purchased for the sum of three dollars. It was probably the only horse at Corpus Christi that could have been purchased just then for any reasonable price."

Another officer without a horse was Capt. Daniel P. Whiting of the 7th Regiment, which marched out of Corpus Christi on March 10. Whiting wrote in his memoirs:

> Leading off on foot at the head of my company, I was sorely fatigued on the first day's march. In fact, I was almost broken down by the time we reached Twelve-Mile Motts (up the Nueces River) where we camped. The next day I was less so but very sorry I was only a captain of foot. We

marched 16 miles to Agua Dulce. By the third day, I began to believe I could succeed in the exercise if I continued judiciously. We marched 14 miles to Santa Gertrudis Creek (where the supply depot was established) and on the fourth day, I arrived at camp quite efficient and elastic and afterwards, and throughout the war, I continued my pedestrianism, never mounted, without fatigue or weariness, and many a stout man succumbed where I never faltered.

As the army marched south, a few days out from Corpus Christi, Lt. Grant saw "an immense herd of wild horses that ranged at that time between the Nueces and the Rio Grande. It was seen directly in advance of the head of the column, but a few miles off. The column was halted for a rest and a number of officers, myself among them, rode out two or three miles to the right to see the extent of the herd.

"The country was a rolling prairie and from the higher ground the vision was obstructed only by the earth's curvature. As far as the eye could reach to our right the herd extended. There was no estimating the number of animals in it. I have no idea they could all have been corralled in the state of Rhode Island or Delaware at one time. People who saw the Southern herd of buffalo 15 or 20 years ago can appreciate the size of the Texas band of wild horses in 1846."

Col. William Whistler's 3rd Brigade, which included the 3rd and 4th regiments of infantry, left Corpus Christi on Wednesday morning, March 11. Lt. W. S. Henry, in the 3rd regiment, wrote in his diary: "We're off for the Rio Grande!"

Henry said the day was scorching hot as they marched up the river over a hog wallow ("because of its boggy nature") prairie. Some commotion was created at the front of the column, Henry said, when two wild javelina hogs were shot. "One of the hogs, after being shot, made for the column and was knocked down by one of the men with the butt of his gun; and a mustang, taking it into his head to be a little restive, relieved himself of his load, a demure-looking camp-woman. After a march of 16 miles (that first day), we camped on the Nueces."

Next day, he wrote, they traveled west over more "hog wallow prairies" and because the roads were so heavy, they marched only eight miles before they camped.

Gen. Taylor, who was marching with the 3rd Brigade, decided to move on ahead, hoping to catch up with Col. Worth's 1st Brigade, which was four days' ahead.

On March 13, three days from Corpus Christi, Henry said they turned southwest, crossed the Agua Dulce Creek, marched another 11 miles and camped at a small creek called Los Pintos[*] with some water holes skirted with heavy timber. The night sky in March 1846 (we are reliably informed), far from the glow of any city lights, would have appeared as black velvet with stars flashing as brilliant diamond points.

On March 14 they saw an immense herd of wild mustangs in the distance and several officers (Capt. Charles May and Lt. Randolph Ridgely, among others) gave chase.

"Mounted on their blooded horses," wrote Henry, "they soon ran up to them. The mustang cannot compare, in either fleetness or endurance, with ours. While halting to 'noon' it, one of the officers came into camp, having by his side a very young colt, which he was leading with a rope. When it became known that it was a wee thing only a few days old, a universal cry was raised against his inhumanity. Another officer jumped on a horse and carried it in the direction of the wild drove and left it near a pond, and it is to be hoped the mother found it."

Lt. Samuel G. French said on the third day of the march,

---

[*] Los Pintos Creek, near today's Banquete.

when they camped a pony he had bought for his servant to ride was bitten on the head by a rattlesnake.

"The animal was treated with ammonia and whisky. The next morning his head was so swollen that I left him behind. A servant of the paymaster, when the infantry came along, found the pony and brought it on to the Rio Grande and returned it to my servant."

On the march south, French said, many of the dragoons and officers on horseback carried a small pole to use to kill rattlesnakes to let their horses graze.

Sarah Bourjett, the Great Western, left Corpus Christi driving a mule-cart loaded with supplies for the mess of Capt. Whiting of the 7th Regiment.

"When we halted for rest and lunch," Whiting later wrote, "we partook of the needful cold bite and refreshment during the march. Considerable game was seen and killed by the hunters and for the first time our mess had a peccary (javelina), a species of small wild hogs that are very fierce and dangerous when wounded. The meat was over-pungent and not much relished.

South of the Santa Gertrudis Creek, Whiting said they halted for a rest.

"Some wild cattle were seen and several riders gave chase and among them a soldier mounted on a pony, servant to one of our captains," Whiting wrote. "He overtook one of the animals, a feisty little longhorn bull with a wild look in his eye, which ran in the direction of the reclining men, and when close at hand ran along parallel to the column, the pursuer on the opposite side endeavoring to head him off. At this moment the man fired his gun, and, missing the beast, the ball struck the ground amidst the soldiers, miraculously hitting no one. Much abuse was visited upon him for his carelessness and stupidity. After we were camped that night, an altercation was heard in this man's tent between himself and his wife, a laundress. Both were Irish. She was heard to say, 'Look at you! What a pretty soldier! Shoot at a bull and miss a regiment!' "

Capt. George A. McCall of the 4th Infantry said they saw an abundance of wild game on the march: "I chased the wild horse and antelope, and killed the wild bull and the wild boar. The Mexican wild boar (javelina) is a singular animal. It has no tail and has a musk-pouch on the after-part of the back, which exudes a strong smell of musk.

"I obtained permission one day to ride off from the column and fell in with a party of eight of these gentlemen," McCall wrote in a letter to his brother. "We had quite a conflict. A large boar charged at me twice with the noise and speed of a small locomotive, but I so managed my horse as to avoid him and, using musket-balls in my double gun, I continued to fire and load, sometimes pursuing and again keeping aloof, till in the course of half a mile I shot down three of them.

"I rode with Col. Garland one morning in advance of the column and we fell in with a large bull who charged us. The Colonel got the first shot, but made a clear miss; and as the bull turned towards him, his horse bolted and ran away with him. As my horse stood perfectly still, I fired from my right barrel a musket-ball, as he arrived within 20 paces of me.

"He was coming at me full tilt and my ball struck him in the forehead, where I had aimed, but a little too low, being planted just over the right eye, whereupon the bull reeled and fell upon his knees. He rose again, but retreated, and I was compelled to follow him at half speed, and to put three more balls into him before he gave up.

"I took his tongue and the meat from one side; but left some six or seven hundred pounds of beef for the wolves and vultures. His tail, which I took as a trophy, I gave to Capt. Bragg, whom I happened to meet as I entered the camp, and with it a good steak."

CHAPTER 14

Crossing the Arroyo Colorado

In the middle of March, as Zachary Taylor's army moved south to the Rio Grande, they traveled into a hot arid country, a dead-looking land known as the sand belt, or "The Sands," then consisted of a region of no trees, no good water, and often with searing heat. Gen. Filisola's army traveled across this harsh land after the Mexican army's defeat at San Jacinto 10 years before.[*]

For Taylor's soldiers, like Filisola's, it was rough marching country, with intense heat, combined with lack of water, that made heads swim and limbs ache.

Lt. Ulysses S. Grant wrote that ponds of drinkable water were sometimes a day's march apart. As the army struggled through this bleak terrain, "a Sahara-like land," Grant admired the endurance of the enlisted men. It really was a scorched-earth place, since, in some places Indians or Mexicans "had burned the herbage. The light ashes, raised by the tramp of many feet, settled on the soldiers' faces till they could scarcely recognize one another. Tortured with thirst, they would occasionally break ranks pell-mell at the sight of water; but as a rule they found it brackish."

---

[*] The sand belt, or "The Sands," 65 miles wide and 100 miles long, had to be crossed traveling by land from Corpus Christi to Brownsville. This harsh, desert-like terrain was known by the Mexicans as "El Desierto de los Muertos," the desert of the dead.

Surgeon N. S. Jarvis noted in his diary that they emerged from a belt of mesquite and entered a region of sandy soil covered with thin grass. "We have now entered upon that part of the country called the desert, the only water found in the distance of 30 miles being mostly salt and the men suffering greatly from thirst, in addition to the heat and dust." The next day, he wrote, proved the most fatiguing march they had yet encountered, both to man and beast:

> This arose from thirst, heat and dust. Our route was southeast over a barren and sandy prairie intersected with numerous salt ponds. Not a tree or shrub was seen the whole distance and the only fresh water we met with was a small pond accidentally discovered by the artillery in advance and three miles from the place where we camped for the night.
>
> Many of the men had been so exhausted by heat and thirst that they had dropped behind. On our arrival at the pond, men, horses, and dogs rushed indiscriminately into the water to slake their thirst and remained there until it was appeased.

The officers and men being in uniform, wrote Lt. Samuel G. French, "had their lips and noses nearly raw from the sun and winds, and could not put a cup of coffee to their lips until it was cold. I wore an immense sombrero, or Mexican straw hat. On the route I was often told, "When General Taylor comes up you will be put under arrest for wearing that hat." But French adjusted his sombrero and kept going.

Cpl. C. M. Reeves of the 4th Infantry said the part of the prairie they were marching over had been burned by Indians "and a fine, suffocating dust arose from the ashes and sand, which got into our mouths and nostrils, and added to our sufferings. Several dogs belonging to the officers perished for want of water, and it was feared that some of the horses would likewise die.

"In the midst of our choking thirst it seemed as if the fates had turned against us. About noon, when man and beast were nearly exhausted, we came in sight of two small and beautiful lakes. 'Thank God!' — 'Good! Good!' — 'Now we'll drink!' was shouted out by the poor men, as each company came in sight of those glorious lakes — 'Water! Water!' was the cry, and as it passed to the rear, 'Water! My God! Water!' was heard from a thousand parched throats.

"The men began to quicken their pace; they broke their ranks in their haste to get to the delicious liquid. The officers tried to preserve order, but they might as well have tried to have stopped a herd of wild buffaloes. Each man rushed forward regardless of his neighbor, and ere they were within several hundred yards of the lakes a thousand tin cups had suddenly been unstrapped and fiercely clutched, ready to dip in the precious element. On we go. Now we ascend the little hillock on the edge of the lake and down we rush madly, blindly, into the sparkling fluid, and jump in where there will be no trouble to get our cups full.

"We dip — we raise it hurriedly and nervously to our mouths, Ye Gods! we drink! No, we don't! It chokes us; we can't swallow that stuff. 'What is that?' said an old soldier, with a shocked look on his face, who in his hurry had let some go down, and ere he had spoken the whole truth flashed on our minds. SALT! And so much so that pure salt had collected on the edge of the lake. 'Don't drink, men, don't drink!' I shouted out to those behind us but they all had to taste for themselves before they would believe it. If those lakes had never before been the cause of any profanity, I think that on this occasion they received their full share. What bitter curses were poured upon them. We sullenly resumed our march and moved on for about four miles when we came to a hole of rainwater, full of animal manure, but it tasted most delicious and I drank four cups, filled to the brim, without stopping."

Lt. E. Kirby Smith of the 5th Regiment wrote:

Our route today was over a sandy desert that was very hard on the men. The ox-teams were not able to keep up. We encamped at a place called Filisola's Wells. Filisola was one of Santa Anna's generals and commanded the rear division at the battle of San Jacinto. He retreated after that battle and rested his army some days at this place.

On the following day, we made a long march over a perfect desert, the scanty herbage having been burnt by the enemy. The only water we saw was salt and the sun streamed upon us like living fire. We were enveloped in clouds of black sooty dust and ashes, which adhered to our beards and skins moist with perspiration. Our own wives would not have known us. Late in the afternoon we halted at a muddy pool of brackish water. After washing and getting a cup of tea, our cheerfulness was restored. On March 16, we started at seven in the morning, the rear of our baggage train still many miles behind. The country today rapidly improved and we encamped early on a rich prairie, surrounded by pleasant woods. Directly in front of our camp was a pond of clear sweet water. Oh, how we did drink and bathe! I never knew before how good water could be after being without it 36 hours. The men all drank and filled themselves up like camels.

Ten days after the march began, the lead elements of Taylor's army began to approach the Arroyo Colorado, which the soldiers called the Little Colorado. The first to arrive were Twiggs' 2nd Dragoons, which left Corpus Christi on Sunday, March 8. As each of the four columns, separated by a day's march, arrived, the army began to re-form near the stream, as Taylor advised the war department in a dispatch, "to be prepared for contingencies."

After crossing the Sands, the soldiers got all the water they could drink, bathed in the stream, and rested their sore feet.

Next day, March 19, a reconnaissance was conducted and a small body of irregular cavalry composed of militia or Mexican rancheros was seen on the other side. They made no hostile moves but told the officer in charge (of the reconnaissance) that any attempt to cross the arroyo would be resisted with gunfire.

Lt. U. S. Grant said they could clearly hear bugle calls from the other side of the arroyo. Gen. Taylor sent Capt. Joseph Mansfield across to talk with the Mexicans, who repeated the warning that any attempt to cross would be opposed. Excitement sparked through the column; some of the faces showed apprehension while others showed excitement that they were likely to meet resistance.

Taylor ordered two batteries moved up to command the crossing. He had engineers cut down the high embankment to make the fording site more accessible. Worth's 1st Brigade with the 2nd Brigade on the right were moved up.

Lt. W. S. Henry wrote, "When Gen. Taylor, with his command, reached the bank of the Arroyo Colorado, Mexican bugles sounded for some distance up and down the river. A fight appeared to be certain, and although our gallant fellows had made up their mind they would have to cross amid a shower of bullets, they were eager to advance. The men were employed cutting down the bank for the passage of the train. Taylor, standing on the bank, told them that "as soon as he cut down the bank he intended to cross and that the first Mexican he saw after our men entered the water would be shot."

About this time "an awful din was heard on the Mexican side by a series of bugle calls," said Lt. French. "Our (battery) guns were loaded and matches were lit when the general gave the command for the infantry to cross."

It was a quarter past nine on the morning of March 20, wrote Capt. E. Kirby Smith of the 5th Infantry. "We deployed on the right of the 1st Brigade on the bank of the arroyo. For the last two miles before we reached the river we met staff officers and camp followers riding to the rear, all with anxious faces warning us that the Mexicans were in force on the opposite bank. As we deployed, we saw a few rancheros and lancers on the other side. This was perhaps one of the most exciting hours of my life. All, from the general-in-chief to the smallest drummer boy, felt morally certain we were on the verge of a bloody conflict, yet I saw no one who was not cheerful and eager for the game to begin."

At half-past 10, four companies of the 2nd Brigade under the command of Capt. C. F. Smith waded into the arroyo. Gen. Worth rushed to lead the charge. "We watched them in breathless silence," wrote E. Kirby Smith, "as they deepened in the water, expecting that at every step they would receive a withering fire. When they were halfway over and not a shot had been fired, the disappointment of the men was revealed in muttered curses." When the column reached the other side of the arroyo, there were cheers and soon one of the regimental bands struck up a flourish of "Yankee Doodle":

> *Father and I went down to camp*
> *Along with Captain Gooding*
> *There were all the men and boys*
> *As thick as hasty pudding.*

A few Mexicans were seen riding away "and the battle of Arroyo Colorado was terminated." Lt. Grant said the threat posed by the Mexican irregulars reminded him of the two wolves howling near Goliad.

"There are always more of them before they are counted."

Camp was broken on March 23 and Taylor's soldiers began their movement toward the Rio Grande. Capt. E. Kirby Smith of the 5th Regiment wrote to his wife: "We presented today an imposing spectacle as we moved in parallel columns across the open prairie, with our long baggage train close to our rear and our scouts far in advance and on our flanks examining every thicket. A thousand rumors were in the mouths of our newsmongers, of forces in our front ready to eat us without pepper or salt."

"There is a physique and morale about our little army of which they never dreamed," Lt. Henry wrote. "It is "well-clad, well-fed, and well-armed, moving forward with an enthusiasm and sangfroid which carries victory" in its face. "I feel more and more convinced that we can successfully contend with an immensely superior force."

The prospect of war was a subject of inexhaustible conversation. Gen. Taylor, before leaving Corpus Christi, published Order No. 30, which was translated into Spanish and sent to be distributed on the border with reassurances that his movement was peaceful in intent and action:

"The Army of Occupation of Texas being now about to take a position upon the left bank of the Rio Grande, under the orders of the Executive of the United States, the General-in-Chief desires to express the hope that the movement will be advantageous to all concerned, and with the object of attaining this laudable end, he has ordered all under his command to observe with the most serious respect the rights of all the inhabitants who may be found in peaceful prosecution of their respective occupations, as well on the left as on the right side of the Rio Grande. Under no pretext nor in any way will any interference be allowed with the civil rights or religious principles of the inhabitants, but the utmost respect for them will be maintained."

Col. Hitchcock noted in his diary: "Since crossing the Colorado we hear a multitude of reports of the most contradictory character. At one moment we hear of a large force crossing the Rio Grande at Matamoros to destroy us; then we hear that the people are in favor of our approach and everything is quiet.

"We hear that 700 men are on our rear and have been following us for several days. They have not been anxious to overtake us, for we have moved slowly. I have been very much prostrated in strength — never was so weak and now I can scarcely hold my pencil to write legibly."

Capt. Daniel P. Whiting of the 7th Infantry wrote that shortly after they resumed the march toward the border, "not knowing whether our advance would be opposed or not, and while crossing an extensive prairie, the brigades were moving in parallel columns about 100 yards apart when an unprecedented incident occurred. Directly in front of our column, advancing at a regular trot to meet us, was a polecat.

"The men at the head of the column shunned the collision and opened to the right and left to admit the animal's free passage, while the utmost consternation pervaded in the crowded ranks.

"The skunk passed through, on business of his own, unheeding the uproar and confusion, while no one dared hinder his progress. All danger past, the brave warriors resumed their onward march and discipline, but for some minutes the army had been utterly routed by a polecat."

CHAPTER 15

First Blood

In the last week of March, 1846, Gen. Taylor issued orders for the army to march to Point Isabel* to secure his base of supplies. On the march the dragoons were on the right and the 3rd Brigade on the left. Lt. W. S. Henry described the land as rich and picturesque, with mesquite and acacia thickets "fragrant with blossoms." They passed by freshwater ponds, and saw ducks, plover, and jackrabbits. The jackrabbits were so fast, Henry wrote, few dogs could catch them.

A rumor swept the column that Point Isabel, their base of supplies, had been attacked and the houses burned. Taylor changed his orders. Taylor and the dragoons were to proceed to Point Isabel while Gen. Worth and the 3rd Brigade would march in the direction of Matamoros.

On the way to Point Isabel a mule was bitten by a rattlesnake. "The whole country is overrun with them," said Henry, who overheard the teamster consoling his mule with words about the fairest always being taken first, "when he well knew his was the ugliest mule in the army."

Taylor arrived at Point Isabel to discover the rumor was unfounded. About the same time steamboats arrived with supplies. Taylor ordered defensive works started to protect

---

* A small village at Point Isabel, a point of the mainland at Brazos Santiago, was called El Frontón de Santa Isabel. Taylor's soldiers referred to Point Isabel and "Frontone" interchangeably.

Point Isabel and led the dragoons back to join Gen. Worth, who was camped eight miles from Matamoros at a place called Palo Alto. The camping ground, said Henry, was a beautiful site, like an English country lawn. The soldiers called the place "Gen. Worth's Camp" but it would later gain a more indelible name.

On March 28 they started for the Rio Grande and reached the river about 11 a.m., where the noonday sun was flooding the river with flecks of gold. Col. William Belknap of the 8th Regiment had a pole cut from a mesquite tree erected as a flag pole on the bank of the river.

The Stars and Stripes was raised while the regimental bands played "Hail Columbia" and "Yankee Doodle": *Father and I went down to camp / Along with Captain Gooding / There were all the men and boys / As thick as hasty pudding.*

The flag was saluted, wrote Capt. Whiting of the 7th Regiment, "to the great indignation of the good people of Matamoros." A large crowd had lined up at the ferry landing, along the riverfront, and gathered on the flat roofs of adobe houses to watch the proceedings of the "barbarians of the north."

Hoisting the flag was a clear declaration that the land on the left bank was now American territory. Taylor's soldiers could hear the jeers and catcalls across the river.

That afternoon, the soldiers watched as young women in Matamoros came down to the river and, wrote E. Kirby Smith, disrobed without any hesitation and plunged into the stream, naked as fishes, regardless of the numerous spectators on either bank.

"Some of our young officers were in the water opposite them and soon swam towards them, laughing and calling out. The Mexican guards were not, however, disposed to let them come much nearer than the middle of the river, so they returned after kissing their hands to the tawny damsels, which was laughingly returned."

142

Near the end of the day, Lt. W. S. Henry wrote, the soldiers were amused when a rooster brought from Corpus Christi by an officer, stood atop a wagon on the riverbank and flapped his wings and crowed, as if in defiance.

Taylor's soldiers made camp in a newly ploughed cornfield. The corn was about six inches high and the furrowed field, said one officer, was not so easy to walk on as the sandy beach at Corpus Christi. They slept near their guns because there were rumors of a night attack, but the night passed without incident and the soldiers slept like blocks. W. S. Henry said the Mexicans had missed at least two good opportunities to initiate a fight: at the crossing of the Arroyo Colorado and that night in the cornfield across from Matamoros.

Capt. Philip N. Barbour of the 3rd Infantry said nearly all the houses on the Texas side of the river (the left bank) were deserted, the residents having crossed the river for safety. "A few families, however, remained on this side and are now reaping the reward of their wisdom by selling in our camp poultry, milk and vegetables."

T. B. Thorpe, who wrote "Our Army on the Rio Grande," noted that the inhabitants of the surrounding country "visited our encampment, offering for sale fresh meats and vegetables. Among these traders, it was said there were Mexican officers in disguise, which was no doubt the case. The residents of the city (of Matamoros) and its troops were continually showing themselves upon the bank of the river, many of the former appearing in open carriages. The narrowness of the Rio Grande gave to these displays quite a social character and made our troops acquainted with the inhabitants of Matamoros. Conversation was carried on across the river, and most amusing protestations of friendship were thus sometimes made."

On the last day of March, rain came down in a steady drizzle. Two men were shot trying to desert by swimming across the river. The shooting of deserters trying to swim across the Rio Grande became an almost daily occurrence. Some of them, it was supposed, were not so much trying to desert to the other side as they were in search of wine, women and song in the fleshpots of Matamoros.

Col. Hitchcock back in December wrote a letter of protest called a "memorial" objecting to giving precedence to brevet rank over seniority. It was signed by 158 officers at Corpus Christi, from Col. Twiggs down to second lieutenants. On April 2, Hitchcock wrote that, "The President of the United States has decided the brevet question on the basis of Gen. Jackson's decision of 1829, and in accordance with our numerously signed memorial. The order was brought me and I read it aloud to all the officers who, knowing that I wrote it, gathered rapidly around to rejoice and congratulate me. It is a signal triumph of justice: we of the line have gained our point completely."

On the third day of April work began building a battery opposite Matamoros. By the sixth of April the battery was completed for four 18-pounders and the guns placed bearing "directly on the public square of Matamoros." Two days later ground was broken behind the battery for a fortified enclosure of six bastions capable of holding up to 2,000 men.

Lt. U. S. Grant said the fort was laid out by the engineers but the work was done by all of Taylor's soldiers, with spade and wheelbarrow, "under the supervision of their officers, the chief engineer retaining general direction." The chief engineer who designed the fort and supervised its construction was Capt. Joseph Mansfield of the engineer corps. Lt. Meade, also of the engineer corps, said Mansfield "deserves a great credit for the design and execution of the work." The fieldwork was called Fort Texas.

By the fourth day of April, Capt. Barbour of Kentucky noted that the army had lost about 30 men by desertion to the enemy. "One of them I understand came back last night and reports that he was offered his choice to serve in the army against us or be sent off to the mines. He relished neither option so he came back. Several slaves belonging to officers have left their masters and gone over to Matamoros. Capt. Richard Gatlin and Lts. Braxton Bragg and Levi Gantt have each lost a boy. If we are located on this border much longer, we shall have to employ white servants."

Lt. Henry said they found no little amusement in a Matamoros newspaper, which reported that the "barbarian army" had lost 43 soldiers and six slaves to desertion "and they expect momentarily old Taylor, body and soul. When they do get him, they will have a bitter pill to swallow."

If the Matamoros newspaper was full of bluster about making short work of the "barbarians of the north," the New Orleans papers warned that Gen. Taylor had placed his little army in mortal danger. One officer wrote that, "You will believe me when I tell you that this army will have the damned hardest fighting that ever an army had in this world. I tell you, the enemy have been entirely underrated and this army has put itself in a trap."

In his diary, Col. Ethan Allen Hitchcock shared something of the same opinion. "Our force is altogether too small for the accomplishment of its errand. It looks as if the government sent a small force on purpose to bring on a war, so as to have a pretext for taking California and as much of this country as it chooses; for, whatever becomes of this army, there is no doubt of a war between the United States and Mexico. My heart is not in this business; I am against it from the bottom of my soul as a most unholy and unrighteous proceeding; but, as a military man, I am bound to execute orders."

A norther, with heavy rain, hit during the early evening of April 8. "In every direction the tents were overthrown and their contents scattered in the mud," wrote E. Kirby Smith of the 5th Regiment to his wife. "My own company had almost entirely disappeared, a few despairing wretches, groping about in the mud for their weapons, was all that was left. The fires were extinguished and desolation reigned in the camp, which was inches deep in standing water, and the men all soaked to the skin."

On April 10, Col. Hitchcock, who had long been sick and looked it, asked for two months' leave of absence for his health. "Col. Twiggs called this morning and expressed his surprise that I had not gone long ago, and particularly that I allowed myself to be 'dragged along through the country' as I did — alluding to my leaving Corpus Christi with the army when sick and travelling a number of days in an ox-wagon. The General has given the order for my leave of absence for 60 days." He left for New Orleans from Point Isabel two days later.

As work proceeded on the fort, on April 10, Col. Trueman Cross, deputy quartermaster general of the army, left camp for his usual morning ride and just disappeared. No one knew where he was or what had happened to him.

When he did not return, Lt. Henry, "fearful apprehensions began to be felt for his safety, as the country was known to be full of rancheros, or irregular cavalry, who were prowling about for plunder and spared neither age nor rank. Towards evening cannon were fired to direct him, if lost, and parties rode out to search for him. Letters were also sent to the commandant at Matamoros to inquire for him, but no intelligence could be obtained."

As search parties were mounted, Col. Cross's son, who served as one of his clerks, was distraught with worry.

The day after Cross disappeared, on April 11, Americans heard the ringing of church bells across the river. As they soon learned, this signaled the arrival of Gen. Pedro de Ampudia, commander in chief of Mexico's Fourth Military District, to take command. Besides the tolling of church bells, his coming was marked with the firing of a salute, a parade of troops, along with "a proportionate barking of dogs."

Ampudia had a brutal reputation. Years earlier in Yucatan, in one of Mexico's frequent revolts, Ampudia's adversary fell into his hands and, as one historian related, "he had his head cut off and boiled in oil and his body mutilated beyond recognition." But despite that reputation, American captives held by Ampudia during the Mexican War said he treated them with the utmost kindness and respect.

One of Ampudia's first acts was to order all American citizens in the city to evacuate inland to Ciudad Victoria to prevent their forming a sympathetic fifth column to aid and support the American army. He next sent a message to Gen. Taylor giving him 24 hours "to break up your camp and return to the east bank of the Nueces River while our governments are regulating the pending question in relation to Texas. If you insist upon remaining upon the soil of the Department of Tamaulipas, it will certainly result that arms, and arms alone, must decide the question."

Only days later, Ampudia was relieved of command and replaced by Gen. Mariano Arista, appointed to command the Army of the North.* Taylor was kept informed of events across the river by Chipito Sandoval, Henry Kinney's friend and spy who accompanied the army south and served on Taylor's staff as a "scout."

By mid-April the whole command was at work on the fort. A number of deserters were shot or drowned trying to cross the river and several slaves of officers escaped to Matamoros. Search parties continued to scour the country for Col. Cross.

Capt. Whiting was excited when his brother-in-law, Lt. Napoleon Jackson Tecumseh Dana, returned after being

---

* When Santa Anna returned to the presidency, Ampudia was restored to commander in chief, just in time to lose the battle of Monterrey.

home on leave. Dana was married to Sue Sanford, the older sister of Whiting's wife. "He arrived in camp from the States, conveying to me Indie's daguerreotype (his wife was Indiana Sanford Whiting). Next best to seeing herself, it cheered my heart and revived my spirits."

Capt. Philip N. Barbour in a letter to his wife dated April 17th that he saw "some Mexican officers pretty tight this afternoon. Understand it is payday with them. Their men each receive a dollar for a month's pay, as we are informed by a Mexican."

Lt. Theodoric Porter, whose acting ability did not extend to being able to kiss U.S. Grant as Desdemona, was killed on April 19 while he was out searching for Col. Cross.

Two days later, a Mexican arrived in camp and said he knew where the body an American officer could be found. The body was lying in a thicket by the road leading down to the river. It was Col. Cross. He had been stripped of clothing and flesh had been ripped away by vultures.

An enquiry by a board of officers determined that he had been attacked and stripped by guerrillas (bandits) of Ramon Falcon* and was killed by a shot to the head. He was buried three days later with an escort of dragoons and eight companies of infantry. W. S. Henry described the scene:

> The procession, under the circumstances, was painfully imposing. First came the infantry, next the dragoons, next the body, drawn by six horses, on the wheels of a caisson; enveloped in the flag of his country; next a sad mourner, his son; then a horse clad in mourning, led by two dragoons, followed by all the officers off duty. The march was so conducted that part of the way it could be seen from the city (across the river). The grave

---

* Bandit leader Ramon Falcon was captured by American forces near Saltillo and hanged on Dec. 19, 1847.

was dug at the foot of the flagstaff.[*] The flag was at half-mast. Colonel Childs read the service for the dead; three volleys were fired, the flag was run up, the escort marched off to a gay and lively tune, and left the dead in silence. Such is a military funeral. We have no time for grief.

In the last week of April, the new fort was mostly finished except for a sally port and the rear face. Rumors reached Gen. Taylor that large Mexican forces had crossed the river some miles below and 20 miles above the fort. Taylor dispatched two squadrons of dragoons to reconnoiter. No sign of the enemy was found below the fort.

The other squadron, under the command of Capt. Seth B. Thornton, rode some 20 miles above the fort. Their guide left them; he warned that a large Mexican force was nearby and he feared being captured. They came to a farm, or hacienda, enclosed in a large mesquite fence. They rode into the enclosure, looking for someone around the buildings to question. An alarm was sounded, the gate closed, and a large force of Mexican infantry began firing at the trapped dragoons from three sides.

Capt. W. J. Hardee told Thornton that their only hope was to tear down the fence and cut their way through to the river. Before they could put this plan into effect, Thornton's horse spooked and ran off with him, clearing the fence in a desperate leap. Hardee surrendered, along with 46 dragoons. Six of them were wounded; seven had been killed. The prisoners were marched in triumph through the streets of Matamoros. Thornton had also been

---

[*] Col. Cross's body was disinterred in November 1846, removed to Washington, D.C., and reburied in the Congressional Cemetery.

captured when his horse fell and rendered him unconscious.*

The 7th Infantry was assigned to garrison the fort along with Capt. Allen Lowd's company of 2nd Artillery, in charge of the four 18-pounder guns, and Lt. Braxton Bragg of the 3rd Artillery with a light battery of four pieces. In command was Maj. Jacob Brown, with orders to conserve his ammunition and defend the fort to the last man. Gen. Taylor ordered the remainder of the army to march to Point Isabel, 27 miles away, to procure supplies, especially ammunition for the guns at the new fort.

On May 1, at 2 p.m., the army left for Point Isabel and marched until midnight. They camped on the broad prairie and, Capt. Barbour wrote, "slept on the ground without fire, water or blankets and feel today very much fatigued and hungry, having had no coffee since yesterday morning and very little of anything else. At this place we found oranges and lemons and everything refreshing except good water." After sleeping on wet ground and waking up cold, they marched on to Point Isabel, which they reached at noon on the following day.

On May 3, they could clearly hear the sound of cannon fire from the direction of the fort and knew the 7th, left to garrison the fort, was under attack. When the rest of the army marched away to Point Isabel, they left their baggage at the fort. Lt. George Gordon Meade wrote his wife that "we were obliged to leave all our baggage in the fort and in my trunk I left your miniature. I very much fear some impudent shell has blown you up, and you will have been in action before myself."

Next day, Gen. Taylor received reports that there had been an exchange of artillery fire between the fort and the

---

* Thornton and other prisoners were freed when Mexican forces abandoned Matamoros.

Mexican batteries across the river but that the enemy shells had done little damage.

Back at the fort, when the firing from the Mexican batteries began, Lt. Forbes Britton ran to his tent, grabbed his rifle, and ran out, just as a nine-pound ball wrecked his tent before it smashed into the parapet. Shells filled with shrapnel exploded in the fort, making a thin whining noise. One shot followed another, then another . . .

Capt. Daniel P. Whiting was washing his face when a round shot passed over from the Mexican side. Whiting rushed out to find men running to get ready for an attack. As Whiting's company was forming, a bomb hit the ground nearby, the fuse burning, and Whiting and his men threw themselves on the ground:

> No sooner had we done so than the shell exploded, tearing up the ground for several yards, but all the fragments flying upward cleared the fort without further injury. The next minute grapeshot struck a sergeant near me on the head; he was never aware of the fatal cause.
>
> Running out, I found the men thronging into position. The men were excited, though they attended to their duties with great coolness and discipline. The ball had opened.
>
> We were in the full experience of a brisk cannonade, with shot and shell, from the Mexican batteries. At the angle of our fort nearest the enemy, the bastion was furnished with a battery of four 24-pounders. It was some three minutes before its commander, Capt. Allen Lowd, was in readiness to reply to the salutation. When Lowd did so, the effect was palpable and satisfactory.
>
> Besides their main battery at the lower end of the city, about 800 yards distant, the Mexicans for some days had been constructing a sand-bag

redoubt at the ferry landing opposite us, about 600 yards off, in which they had placed a single gun of large caliber. We could see its black muzzle with the naked eye from our parapet. From the redoubt, at point blank distance, active discharge was commenced at the same time with the lower battery.

When Capt. Lowd directed one of his 24s at its gaping embrasure, one discharge was sufficient. Gun carriage and Mexican soldiers flew into the air. The redoubt, a shattered wreck, was cleared of its occupants, who were seen flying in hot haste for a safer asylum.

The roar of cannons from the other battery continued while our fort replied for about four hours. Capt. Lowd occasionally delivered an iron messenger from his guns crashing into the city, which we could distinctly hear tearing its course through the houses and streets. At this point, Capt. Lowd, finding he had already consumed half his ammunition with no materially serious effect on the enemy, ceased firing. It was not resumed during the siege, except an occasional gun at some intrusive or inquisitive party in the other directions, from one of the river bastions. Lowd was reserving the remainder of our supply for any contingent necessity.

At the fort that night the soldiers erected bomb-proofs (covered ways for protection against shrapnel) with whatever they could find, including the baggage, bedrolls and belongings of the absent troops.

As bombs were still falling, on the afternoon of May 6, Maj. Jacob Brown, known as a cool and methodical officer, walked around the fort to see that every man was at his post. While he was talking with a soldier, a shell struck a nearby parapet, ricocheted and exploded on the ground, mortally wounding the commander. The blast took off his right leg. He was carried into one of the bomb-proof shelters, where he died three days later. The command devolved to Capt. Edgar Hawkins.

Soon after Major Brown fell, Mexican infantry and cavalry approached the rear of the fort, but they fell back on receiving directed canister fire from Lt. Bragg's battery. From 10 a.m. until shortly after four p.m. the artillery bombardment continued until a delegation bearing a white flag approached, to the sound of bugles, and sought a parley. Lt. Forbes Britton, quartermaster of the 7th Infantry who was on at least working terms with the Spanish language, was sent out to talk. Lt. Britton received a written communication from Gen. Mariano Arista demanding the fort's surrender. Arista's letter said, in part:

You are besieged by forces sufficient to take you and there is, moreover, a numerous division encamped near you which, free from all other cares, will keep off any aid which you may expect to receive. The respect for humanity, acknowledged at the present age by all civilized nations, doubtless imposes upon me the duty of mitigating the disasters of war. This principle, which Mexicans observe above all other nations, obliges me to summon you, as all your efforts will be useless, to surrender, in order to avoid, by a capitulation, the entire destruction of all the soldiers under your command.

Capt. Hawkins, in command of the fort after Major Brown was hit, convened the senior officers (including Capt. Mansfield, the principal engineer, Capt. Whiting of the 7th Infantry and Lt. Bragg of the 3rd Artillery) on how to respond. The vote was unanimous: they would defend the fort to the end. Hawkins' reply to Arista was delivered an hour later:

> Sir: Your humane communication has just been received and, after the consideration due to its importance, I must respectfully decline to surrender my forces to you.

Gen. Arista's forces crossed the river and took a position to block Taylor's return from Point Isabel and cut his line of supply. Arista's pickets could be seen from Fort Texas.

On May 7, with supplies loaded, Taylor started to return to the besieged Fort Texas, traveling over a prairie. The soldiers spent a fitful night, wrote Lt. James Longstreet. They had heard the artillery fire of the day before and knew hostilities were likely the next day. It was a long wakeful night. They hardly slept at all. "The mosquitoes seemed as thick as the blades of grass on the prairie and swarmed and buzzed in clouds, and packs of half-famished wolves prowled and howled about us. There was no need for the sound of reveille. The wolves and mosquitoes, and perhaps some solemn thoughts, kept us on the *qui vive.*"

Next day, in the afternoon, they reached a stand of timber known as Palo Alto to the Mexican soldiers but to the American soldiers it was called Gen. Worth's Camp, where Worth had camped a month before. It was not a place you would remember especially, unless you had a fight there.

On the afternoon of May 8, two months to the day that the army began its march south, Taylor's soldiers came in sight of Gen. Arista's cavalry, their bayonets and bright-work reflecting the sun. Here, at Palo Alto, Taylor's soldiers got their first smell of battle. Lt. Grant described the scene:

> Early in the forenoon of May the 8th, an army,

outnumbering our little force, was seen drawn up in line of battle just in front of the timber. Their bayonets and spearheads glistened in the sunlight. The force was composed largely of cavalry armed with lances. Where we were the grass was tall, reaching nearly to the shoulders of the men, very stiff, and each stock was pointed at the top, and hard and almost as sharp as a darning-needle. General Taylor halted his army before the head of the column came in range of the artillery of the Mexicans.

Taylor then formed a line of battle, facing the enemy. His artillery, two batteries and two 18-pounder iron guns, drawn by oxen, was placed in position at intervals along the line. Orders were given for a platoon of each company to stack arms and go to a stream off to the right of the command, to fill their canteens and also those of the rest of their companies. When the men were all back in their places in line, the command to advance was given. As I looked down that long line of about 2,000 armed men, advancing toward a larger force also armed, I thought what a fearful responsibility Gen. Taylor must feel, commanding such a host and so far away from friends.

They faced a Mexican army of 6,000 men drawn up in line, ready to take up battle, in front of the timber. The first battle of the war was at hand. Taylor gave orders to advance and Gen. Arista's army opened fire with artillery and the American guns replied. During the artillery exchange, the tall grass caught fire and smoke obscured the battlefield. Under this smoke screen Gen. Arista attacked the left of Taylor's line and was driven back by the American artillery. Near sunset, the Mexicans fell back as Taylor's troops advanced.

Another description of this first battle of the Mexican War came from Capt. Philip N. Barbour of the 3rd Infantry, who said his position on the battlefield was such that it enabled him "to see with distinctness what took place on both sides.":

On May 8, the army marched six miles and bivouacked. The following day, at a place known as Gen. Worth's Camp, an advance guard reported the enemy was waiting in a position to our front. Gen. Taylor ordered a halt until the train came up and then the army resumed the march until it came within sight of the Mexican army deployed in line of battle across the road* we were marching on.

Taylor was ready to give battle. He halted the army to allow men to fill their canteens and animals to get water from a small pond. After half an hour, the army deployed in line of battle in front of the chaparral, by the pond. The advance was sounded and the line moved off, starting with the 5th Infantry, Samuel Ringgold's artillery, the 3rd Infantry, 6th Infantry, two 18 pounders, Lt. Col. Thomas Childs' battalion of artillery, James Duncan's artillery, and the 8th Infantry on the extreme left. Two squadrons of cavalry were stationed, with Capt. Croghan Ker's dragoons in the rear with the train and Capt. Charles May's dragoons 200 yards in advance of our line to mark the position at which the general intended to open his batteries.

The enemy's line was drawn up in fine style, its two flanks resting on woods with other woods in its rear. Before we reached Capt. May's position, their batteries opened up and poured in a heavy

_____
* The Point Isabel Road.

156

fire. Our line advanced under it without the slightest confusion up to the position indicated for it to halt.

Duncan's and Ringgold's batteries were thrown forward on the left and right and commenced a terrific fire upon the enemy and immediately after that the 18 pounders in our center opened also. A terrible cannonading was kept up for near an hour from both sides. Our infantry, drawn up in one line, was exposed to it and suffered smartly on the left where the 8th Infantry was in column of divisions and Col. Childs' battalion formed in square.

The 3rd, 4th and 5th Infantry, being deployed in line of battle, suffered little. The enemy's cavalry on their left flank was played upon by Ringgold's battery, on our right, with fine effect and moved off with a battery of artillery to turn our right flank and gain our rear. This demonstration was met by the 5th Infantry being thrown out to check their advance and the 3rd Infantry to support it. The 5th gained a position partially concealed by a sparse growth of chaparral and formed square to receive the shock of the enemy's cavalry. They dashed up towards it but a well-directed fire checked their advance. By this time Lt. Randolph Ridgely with two pieces of Ringgold's battery had gained a favorable position to play upon them and poured in so destructive a fire that they were thrown into confusion and forced to retire with their artillery which was just being planted against our flank when Ridgely opened his fire upon them.

In the meantime, Ringgold with the other two pieces advanced and occupied the ground abandoned by their left flank and raked their cavalry as they returned, which forced them to take position farther to their right. Gen. Taylor now ordered an oblique change of front to sustain Ringgold and take the enemy in flank. This forced the enemy into a corresponding change of front, during which maneuver the firing was suspended on both sides, but reopened with unabated fury when it was completed.

After the change of front, James Duncan moved rapidly to a position not over 300 yards from the enemy's right flank which he gained unperceived under cover of a dense volume of smoke that rolled up from the burning prairie. Duncan opened so unexpected and destructive a fire that their ranks were broken and hundreds of them mowed down and the whole right wing of their army thrown into confusion. This closed the day and the enemy left the field. Our army then moved forward and encamped upon their original line of battle.

A golden sliver of sunshine was left on the horizon as the battle ended and darkness fell. During the night, the moon waxed red as blood and the two armies were close enough, said Lt. Longstreet, to hear the moans of the wounded. There were huddled shadows and shapes on the battlefield that, in the rising dark, were steeped in violent purple. They bivouacked under the stars.

In the day's battle, American casualties were nine killed and 47 wounded while Arista lost 200 men killed and wounded. Among the American casualties was Lt. Jacob E. Blake of the Topographical Engineers. Earlier in the day, before the battle, Lt. Blake had dashed forward alone, made a quick inspection of the Mexican lines before they realized his intent, and reported back to Gen. Taylor. "He was one of the heroes of the day," wrote Longstreet, "but his laurels were enjoyed only a few hours. As he took his pistol off that night and threw it on the ground an accidental explosion of one of the charges gave him a mortal wound."

Major Ringgold of the 3rd Artillery was shot through the thighs by a cannon ball, passing from right to left, and passing through the withers of the horse he was riding. He fell from the saddle and had scarcely reached the ground when one of his lieutenants came to his assistance and called for a caisson to carry him to the rear. Ringgold told him, "Be careful to get an empty caisson; you may require all your ammunition." He died a day later at Point Isabel. Casualties in a battle are soon forgotten but Ringgold's name would be long remembered.

Next day, May 9, Arista retreated and Taylor followed.

Lt. Longstreet said his company was marching on the right side of the road when they came to the body of a young Mexican woman. "She had ceased to breathe but blood heat was still in her body and her expression was lifelike. A profusion of black hair covered her shoulders and person, the only covering to her waist. This sad spectacle, so unlike our thoughts of battle, unnerved us a little." They learned later that Arista's army brought to the field some 500 women to be employed in pillaging and stripping the dead, said Capt. George A. McCall.

At an old channel of the Rio Grande called Resaca de la Palma, Arista's forces formed as Taylor's troops advanced.

Capt. Philip N. Barbour of the 3rd Infantry wrote that, "shortly after daylight the enemy's forces were seen moving in front of the chaparral into which they retired last night. Gen. Taylor called a council of war upon the presentation of Col. Twiggs that the commanders of corps were in favor of entrenching our camp where it was and awaiting reinforcements. It leaked out after the council broke up that seven out of 10 were in favor of this suggestion of inaction. But Col. James McIntosh, Capt. W. W. Morris and Lt. James Duncan, to their praise, were in favor of fighting again. The general sided with them."

Orders were given, wrote Barbour, to entrench the train, along with artillery (two 18 pounders and two 12 pounders) with a small detachment of artillerymen and the teamsters for its defense.

"The army now moved forward," Barbour continued, "to fell the enemy who by this time had disappeared into the chaparral. A reconnaissance of about two hours satisfied Gen. Taylor that they had retreated upon the road we were compelled to pursue. Dispositions were now made to advance.

"Capt. George A. McCall with 200 light troops was sent in advance with Capt. May's squadron to gain intelligence and report to the general. The main body moved forward in one column. After advancing three miles a report was sent back from the advance that the enemy was in position in our front and seemed prepared for battle.

"The general directed Lt. Stephen Dobbins of the 3rd to go forward with a party of McCall's men and draw the enemy fire with a view to ascertain the position of his batteries, while the main body followed close after him. In half an hour Dobbins was saluted with a shower of grapeshot which wounded him and two sergeants of the 3rd Infantry and killed an artillery private. The 8th and 5th Infantries were immediately deployed on the left and perpendicular to the road and the 3rd and 4th in the same way on the right, while Lt. Ridgely's battery was ordered to advance on the road and open upon the enemy.

"In a few minutes the 5th and 8th were engaged with the enemy's infantry while their batteries on both sides of the road continued to pour into the chaparral a deadly fire of grape and canister. Our artillery had no effect upon them and the general ordered Capt. May to charge their position and drive the cannoneers from their guns.

"This was executed with brilliant courage and May brought back Gen. Vega prisoner. The 5th Infantry followed his charge and secured their batteries on the right, keeping up with the 8th a desperate conflict with their infantry. In the meantime, the 3rd and 4th Infantry continued to advance, but owing to the impenetrable nature of the thicket the companies became separated and only detachments such as the officers could pick up at hand were brought into action.

"These, however, did good service," Barbour wrote, "driving the enemy from their guns on the right of the road and piling up their bodies about them. Our artillery now began to have its effect upon them and they commenced giving back. After wandering through the thicket in the hottest of the fire for some time, I succeeded in finding my way out and gained the road, where I met Col. Garland who told me the 3rd was deployed to the right. I pushed on with 12 men of my company, all I could keep together in the thicket, and soon was informed by Capt. Joseph Eaton and Capt. W. W. S. Bliss, whom I met successively, that the 3rd was in the action ahead, to the right of the road.

"I moved forward double-quick, passing under the enemy's fire for 50 yards along the road, crossed the ravine on which they were entrenched and gaining the rising ground on the other side untouched, was just in time to render important service to a detachment of the 4th under lieutenants Christopher Augur, John Richey, and Alexander Hays whom I found retiring before a large body of lancers.

"I united their party to my 12 men and taking a good position in a clear space on the left of the road poured in a galling fire upon the lancers as they came up, and killing three drove the rest back on the road.

"They rallied and returned; my fire checked their advance but three of them went by to rescue a piece of artillery in the hands of a few of our men near the ravine. They were opposed there and driven back and as they passed my command left two of their number to swell the list of dead.

"At this time Ridgely's battery came up and a single discharge upon their cavalry threw it into confusion and the troops on either side of the road, having driven back their infantry, a deafening shout of triumph went up from the whole of our men which struck such terror into the Mexican ranks that they fled in all directions. The pursuit now commenced. On we went, dragoons, artillery and infantry at full run, yelling at every step, which was kept up for three miles, until we reached the Rio Grande and found that the enemy had crossed to the other side, some in boats, some by swimming, while the greater portion ran on up the river, as we afterward learned, and crossed some miles above.

"Never was there a more complete rout or brilliant victory. Our loss was considerable — but nothing like that of the Mexicans, the road and adjacent thickets were filled with their dead. I cannot give particulars as they would fill a volume. My escape was miraculous. It appears like a dream to me. We have captured all the supplies of the Mexican army including eight pieces of artillery, upwards of 1,000 stand of small arms, 20 wagon loads of ammunition, 600 or 700 pack mules, the personal baggage of their officers, and what is more valuable than the rest, Gen. Arista's portfolio, containing the most important information. From the river we returned and slept on the battleground."

Next morning, Capt. Barbour wrote, "We have been engaged all day in burying the dead of both armies." In passing through the Mexican camp after the battle, wrote Capt. McCall, "there was seen every evidence of Gen. Arista's confidence. His property was arranged with great neatness. His own tents and camp-equipage were of the costliest material and his whole dinner service, for instance, was of silver, estimated in value at a thousand dollars. The outfits of the other general officers were also very stylish."

Plunder of every description was brought in, Lt. Edmund Kirby Smith wrote in a letter to his mother, "but every article, from a knife to a twelve-pounder has been delivered up by order of Gen. Taylor; even the very coats our men had on their backs were given up without a murmur, for they lost most of their clothes in the first action."

In the second day's battle, Taylor lost 150 men to 1,200 Mexican soldiers killed or wounded. The field work, pounded by artillery for four days, was saved and the Farmer with Eggs to Sell had won his first two battles of the war. After the battle, Lt. Meade wrote his wife:

> The enemy's loss is tremendous. Their officers acknowledge losing 400 killed and wounded, on the eighth, and we already have buried 100 of their men here, where the affair of the ninth came off, and we have some 50 wounded officers and men. But I must refer you to our official reports, which will show you the number of killed and wounded on both sides, and quantity of property we have taken.
>
> I can now show my face with something to sustain me when I return to Philadelphia. I want to see Matamoros taken, our steamboats established on the river, and every preparation made for advancing into their country. I shall never regret coming here, as I have been connected with events that will be matters of history.

There were happy warriors inside the fort, now that it was all over and they were still alive. Capt. Whiting wrote, "We were crowded with visitors from the camp who were startled at the appearance of the fort. When they had left for Point Isabel, the order and finish were complete, nothing obstructed the interior esplanade. The slopes and grading of the parapet and bastions were perfect from under the supervision of the engineers. When now surveyed, after bombardment from Mexican batteries, the whole interior was plowed and furrowed by exploding bombs, dug up and piled in heaps and ridges amid battered rubbish and bursting baggage. Tents riddled by shot and shell were streaming in tattered ruin. The torn parapets and ragged embankments testified to the vindictiveness of the siege. Gen. Taylor in an order consecrated the services and sacrifices of our late commander, Jacob Brown, by naming our redoubtable field work "Fort Brown".

Whiting recorded several incidents that occurred during the bombardment. When the firing began, "our flag was still located near the bank in front but was not yet raised. My sub, Lt. Earl Van Dorn, volunteered to give it to the wind, but Major Brown remarked that it would be too hazardous. Van Dorn said, "It ought to be elevated, as it will not answer to be fighting without our banner."

"Well, do it then," Brown told Van Dorn. With some volunteers, Van Dorn repaired with the flag to the staff. It was hoisted while every gun in the Mexican batteries bore upon the spot, the balls thickly furrowing the ground about it, but the party retired within the fort again after coolly accomplishing their object, without loss or injury."

Whiting said Sarah Bourjett (the Great Western) "abandoned our mess when the firing began and resorted with the other women and noncombatants to a shelter." *

"During the shelling, chicken coops were knocked open and a chicken was killed by a shell fragment. My valet, an Irishman called Mac, cooked it for my dinner. Afterwards, without waiting for an accident, Mac would serve a fowl for our repast, remarking, whenever a shell burst in the fort, 'There goes another chicken.' So we had our merriment."

---

* Other reports give her more credit. Maj. William Chapman wrote his wife that she "made herself highly useful" during the bombardment. Some accounts say she nursed the wounded, cooked, and delivered coffee and hot food to the men manning the walls. On one of her trips, a shell exploded near her and tore a hole through her bonnet. Whatever the truth was, the stories contributed to the legend of the Great Western.

"The army would never forget in that dark hour which preceded the victories of the 8th and 9th of May, 1846," Lt. Henry wrote, "when our countrymen thought our little army sacrificed. But Gen. Taylor with perfect fearlessness, without a doubt of the result, boldly marched forward, met the enemy's legions, and conquered them, evincing to the world the courage, force, and discipline of our little army."

Perhaps some remembered the probably apocryphal story of Taylor who was mistaken for a farmer and asked, "How's crops, old fellow?" "Oh," he replied, "purty good."

In Washington, President Polk on May 11 asked Congress for a declaration of war based on the ambush of Thornton and Hardee; he was unaware of the battles of Palo Alto and Resaca de la Palma. Congress declared war against Mexico on May 13.

CHAPTER 16

Seen the Elephant

May 18, 1846: More than a week after the battle of Resaca de la Palma Gen. Taylor occupied Matamoros, low-hanging fruit within easy reach across the Rio Grande. Gen. Mariano Arista, after his resounding defeats, pulled out of Matamoros, leaving behind his sick and wounded.

As light companies crossed the river, followed by the regular infantry, Col. Twiggs ordered one of the regimental bands to strike up "Yankee Doodle." (*There were all the men and boys / As thick as hasty pudding.*)

Lt. George Stevens of the 2nd Dragoons was drowned while trying to cross the river with his squadron.[*] Across the river, the American flag was raised from the walls of Fort Paredes, a battery redoubt near the ferry crossing.

Soon after Matamoros was occupied, Lt. Abner Doubleday of the 1st Artillery went to a fandango. The American officers, Doubleday wrote, took off their swords and put them aside so they could dance more freely. Mexican men at the fandango "apparently out of curiosity began examining these weapons and passing them to the rear. A foreigner who was present and understood Spanish and English called out to us that there was a plot to assassinate us with knives and that our swords would soon be lost in the crowd. We came together, drew our pistols, reclaimed our swords, and left in a body."

---

[*] His body was recovered and buried under the flagpole at Fort Brown.

Taylor's troops marched out of Matamoros and into history. They took Camargo in July and in September, after a fierce four-day battle, captured Monterrey, a strong and fortified city. The quarrelsome Gen. Worth, the "Marshal Ney of the Army," was promoted to brevet major general for his part in the victory of Monterrey. Gen. Taylor then took Saltillo without a fight.

Near the ranch house at Buena Vista, American soldiers watched as Mexican soldiers celebrated mass at daybreak before the day's bitter fighting. Of Taylor, Col. Hitchcock had written in his diary, *"If he succeeds, it will be by accident."* In winning decisive victories at Palo Alto, Resaca de la Palma, Monterrey and Buena Vista, Taylor recorded an unbroken string of "accidents".

The U.S. strategy changed by orders from Washington and the seat of war shifted from Gen. Taylor's theater in northern Mexico to Gen. Winfield Scott's landing at Veracruz, for a thrust at Mexico City. Scott's soldiers marched through Veracruz, once again to the regimental fife and drum playing "Yankee Doodle." At Veracruz, city of the true cross, an American colonel bought a parrot whose few words of raucous Spanish, the seller sincerely assured him, translated as, "The damned Yankees are coming! Run! Run!"

On April 8ᵗʰ Gen. Scott began his advance on the city of Mexico by following the route that Hernan Cortez and the conquistadors took three centuries before. After defeating the Mexicans at the mountain pass of Cerro Gordo, at Jalapa, then Puebla, a 13-minute battle at Contreras, where Mexico's Army of the North was all but destroyed, followed by hard-fought battles at Churubusco and Chapultepec. Scott attacked the capital and entered it on Sept. 14, 1847. The army occupied the city of Mexico until the treaty of peace was signed in February 1848.

In the war in Mexico, the U.S. army was much smaller than the Mexican army but it was superior in leadership —

especially with younger West Point trained officer corps — and its artillery. These two factors provided the measure of victory at Palo Alto and Resaca de la Palma and then from Monterrey to Mexico City. Another factor was the time the army spent in encampment at Corpus Christi, from the first day of August 1845 until March 8, 1846.

Oliver Otis Howard, later a major general in the army, wrote that while the army was at Corpus Christi, Gen. Taylor instilled the discipline, drill, organization and social cementing the army needed to succeed.

"It became strong and conscious of its strength under the leader the soldiers believed in. This was an esprit de corps hard to produce but, when produced, hard for a foe to face and overcome."

Capt. Daniel P. Whiting of the 7th Infantry reflected on what the army gained during its seven months of concentration and training at Corpus Christi. One beneficial influence, Whiting wrote, "was the opportunity afforded for fraternity and unlimited association between officers of different corps. Here all sectionality and jealousy of feeling was overcome. A general harmony and mutual consideration acquired and cultivated. This essentially contributed to the unity of feeling and generosity of estimation so elevating to the soldier and ameliorating in his career, and from which association and fraternization may be dated that good feeling and esprit de corps that afterwards prevailed throughout the war."

TWO YEARS EARLIER, BEFORE the war was begun and terminated, when Hitchcock's 3rd Infantry marched away from Corpus Christi on March 11, 1846, W. S. Henry looked back at the site where Taylor's army had camped for the past seven months. *"The fields of white canvas were no longer visible and the campground looked like desolation itself. But the bright waters of the bay looked as sweet as ever."*

The largest concentration of the U.S. Army in one place since George Washington's time marched away. Those in the town who made their living from the army also left. The town just emptied out except for a small nucleus of traders, their families and employees. They had numbered an estimated 100 to 200 when the army arrived, then the town grew to some 2,000 people with a populace, besides the traders, of adventurers, gamblers, saloon-keepers, prostitutes and the many camp followers of a large army outpost.

Gen. Taylor had warned in the army's marching orders, which were reprinted in the "Corpus Christi Gazette," that, "no person not properly attached to it will be permitted to accompany the troops." Despite those orders, some managed to make their way south, traveling separately or along with the baggage train of the army.

Grog-shop purveyors packed up their barrels of whisky and followed the army. On Santa Gertrudis Creek, which would later become the site of King Ranch headquarters, an army depot was established. Some of the saloon-keepers with freight wagons filled with whisky were arrested at Santa Gertrudis. Their liquor was dumped out and they went sent back to Corpus Christi in irons.

The "Houston Telegraph" took note of Corpus Christi's decline from a prominent place frequently mentioned in national news to a suddenly empty village:

> Since the removal of the U.S. Army from Corpus Christi, the town has fallen almost as rapidly as it rose. The population has dwindled from nearly 2,000 souls to a few hundred. The 200 grog shops that were the glory of the citizens a few weeks since, the faro banks, roulette tables, have disappeared and a few stores are about all that is left of the late flourishing town of Corpus Christi.

Even the town's founder, Henry Kinney, left with the army. He was appointed to the staff of Gov. James P. (Pinckney) Henderson in command of Texas troops. Kinney, with the rank of major, served as division quartermaster, procuring goods and supplies for the Texas volunteers. Kinney's business partner, William Aubrey, went south with a wagonload of expensive spirits — Dicky Jones brandy, Madeira wine, and Monongahela whiskey — which he advertised for sale on the border.

After the battles of Palo Alto and Resaca de la Palma followed by the occupation of Matamoros, the grog-shop owners who had been at Corpus Christi were in business again.

Samuel Bangs, the pioneer printer from Boston and publisher of the "Corpus Christi Gazette," packed up his type trays and joined the exodus "to get closer to the seat of conflict." He was soon printing "The American Flag" in Matamoros with some of the same advertising customers he had served in Corpus Christi. One ad in the "Flag" said, "Mr. and Mrs. Brown, late of Corpus Christi, are prepared to accommodate boarders by day or week at the United States House in Matamoros."

Lt. Philip Barbour in a letter to his wife said that "Mrs. Sarah Taylor of Corpus Christi reminiscence has set up her place in Matamoros and is making money hand over fist."

Bangs' "American Flag" kept abreast of what news there was from Corpus Christi. On July 17, 1846, the "Flag" printed a report from an unnamed correspondent who had recently visited the town. It seems most likely that it was written by Henry Kinney, who could visit the town regularly in his quartermaster role with J. Pinckney Henderson's Texas volunteers. It certainly reflects Kinney's interest as the tireless promoter of the town he founded:

According to promise, I write you what information I have been able to gather since my return to Corpus Christi.

I found the old inhabitants of the place, almost to a man, had departed for the Rio Grande, and not only the men, but the women too. Corpus Christi is indeed deserted. But think not that those who have departed, under excitement, will have left us forever. When they have "seen the elephant"* and find that his haunts afford no resting place so lovely and calmly beautiful as this delightful village, they will return.

Later that summer the "American Flag" reported that an unsourced rumor was making the rounds that a Comanche raiding party had attacked Corpus Christi and forced the citizens to "retire for safety to St. Joseph's Island." While the paper said the rumor was probably unfounded, it did note that the town was badly exposed since the departure of the army and many of the town's citizens. "Nearly all the male population of the place are now in Matamoros or upon the Rio Grande," said the paper, "and there are no ranging companies nearer than San Antonio."

Rumors of the attack led Gen. Zachary Taylor to issue orders returning a company of Texas volunteers from Corpus Christi back to protect the exposed town. The company was under the command of Capt. Mabry B. (Mustang) Gray, attached to Samuel H. Walker's First Texas Mounted Riflemen. Gray's rangers, who called themselves Mustangers after their commander, included Andy Walker, Reuben Holbein, David Hatch, Pat Quinn, and William Clark.

At the time Gray's Mustangers were at Corpus Christi, a young soldier from Kentucky, William McClintock, passed through on his way to join the army in Mexico. McClintock wrote in a letter home: "Last night I was introduced to

---

* The phrase was popular during the Mexican War. The expression is defined as meaning to venture forth into the wider world, to gain hard-won experience, to "see the elephant."

Capt. Gray, commandant of the company of Texan rangers stationed near this town. Gray is a fair specimen of the ranger, at all times ready to engage in a fight, foray, amour, dance or drinking bout." Gray's company was ordered back to Camargo.* McClintock wrote in a letter back to Kentucky that:

> The town is on a low beach and contains some 30 houses, and on the hill are 15 or 20 Mexican huts now deserted. Corpus Christi was a poor insignificant place until the army of occupation took up its quarters there last summer. I think its existence will be a short one, since no vessels but those of the smallest size can reach it. The bar blocking the bay is extensive and dangerous. Trade will seek more eligible places.
>
> Capt. Alexander Stevenson, a member of the Legislature, invited me to stay at his house. Stevenson is a native of Philadelphia, but he has been in Texas since 1834 and is now a Southerner in manners and appearances. His lady and her sister are both Texas natives. They are the most interesting and intelligent women I met between the Red River and the Rio Grande. I might add the handsomest and do no injustice.
>
> What struck me with surprise was that these ladies were strongly opposed to the annexation of Texas by the United States. They would have preferred Texas to stand or fall alone . . .
>
> In the evening, Stevenson and I returned from shooting ducks on 'the falls' above the town.* We

---

* Gray's Mustangers soon gained a reputation for conducting a cold-blooded massacre at Rancho Guadalupe near the village of China.

* McClintock may have been referring to the impounded water pond on the bluff known as "Kinney's Tank" below where the Central Library is today, or the Salt Lake a mile west of town.

had fine sport. Earth and water were covered with infinite numbers of ducks, geese, cranes and swans. At the fire of our pieces, they rose in such dense clouds as for a time to darken the air.

In the last week of October 1846, a regiment of cavalry of Tennessee volunteers passed through Corpus Christi on their way to join Taylor's forces in northern Mexico. The Tennesseans rode down the bluff and made their way to Taylor's old encampment, which had been empty since March.

The drainage ditches that divided the campground were spaced for infantry companies and regiments, which made it confining for a large body of cavalry (some 900 men, horses, and a wagon train) so they moved around, like a cat settling in a more comfortable spot, and ended up camping along the shoreline outside the breastworks.

A private in the company, George Furber, who later wrote a book about the war ("The Twelve Months Volunteer"), said a small schooner rode at anchor in front of the town and the town itself consisted of 30 or 40 houses, "one or two quite pretty places. One was the residence of Colonel Kinney, which was a very neat and tastefully fitted-up house, though small."

After they were camped, a quartermaster's detail was sent into town to purchase corn and oats for the horses, but there were only 50 sacks "which gave each horse about five pints." A schooner was sent over to St. Joseph's Island, where the military depot was located, and returned with more forage.

Some of the men took the opportunity to bathe in the bay "and hundreds were in the water, up and down the beach; almost everyone had his horse in, too, and that evening the horses were cleaner than they had been for months. To most of the men, the saltwater was new and when they went in they took soap with them and applied it to their bodies, heads, whiskers. These were presently covered with pure grease, for in putting soap into saltwater the alkali, or potash, of the soap leaves its combination with the grease and unites with the salt acids of the water, and the grease remains upon every article touched with the soap. The heads of some of these men were soon stuck in a mass, with the grease; while others had their fine whiskers, upon which they prided themselves, stuck together. They all soon found that saltwater and soap did not work well together."

Furber said some of the men went into the town and bought whisky "and under its influence made much noise in the night." The Tennesseans discovered that dry mesquite wood "makes as good a fire as our best hickory, and it burns freely, with intense heat, yet lasts well." At noon the next day they decamped to join Taylor's troops at Walnut Springs, near Monterrey.

It was also in October 1846 when Lt. Cadmus M. Wilcox and Lt. William Gardner arrived by steamer from Port Lavaca and landed at the wharf on St. Joseph's Island, on the way to join their regiment, the 4th Infantry, in Mexico. The army's general hospital on the island was still in operation, Wilcox found, where a number of men who were wounded in the battles of Palo Alto and Resaca de la Palma were convalescing. "Several one-legged soldiers were seen hobbling about with crutches."

When the war in Mexico ended in 1848, adventurers and soldiers returned to the Corpus Christi area to settle down. The history of Corpus Christi is filled with the names of soldiers or those connected with the army who returned after the war. Richard King and Mifflin Kenedy, riverboat captains on the Rio Grande who ferried supplies for the army, established ranching empires in the region. Norwick Gussett, a sergeant in U.S. Grant's company in the 4th Infantry, came back after the war to become a wealthy dealer in hides and wool and built the town's second bank. Matthew Dunn, a teamster in northern Mexico, returned to establish a farm northwest of town. Irish orphans Matthew and Thomas Nolan, bugle boys in Twiggs' 2nd Dragoons, returned from Mexico to become Texas rangers and lawmen. Forbes Britton, a quartermaster in the 7th Regiment, came back and entered the Mexican hide-and-wool trade, and was elected to the Texas Senate. Henry Kinney, the town's founder, spent the war as a quartermaster buying beef and other supplies for the army. He returned to Corpus Christi at war's end after a two-year absence, after he, too, had seen the elephant.

The returning soldiers fought in the battles with Zachary Taylor and Winfield Scott and marched through the streets of Matamoros, Monterrey, Saltillo, Veracruz and maybe Mexico City to the strutting and martial tune of "Yankee Doodle":

"Father and I went down to camp
Along with Captain Gooding
There were all the men and boys
As thick as hasty pudding."

APPENDIX 1

Epilogue

Mexican general **Pedro de Ampudia** was appointed general in chief of the Mexican Army of the North before the outbreak of the Mexican War. He was succeeded by Mariano Arista, but fought under him in the battles of Palo Alto and Resaca de la Palma. He regained command and was the commanding officer at the siege and fall of Monterrey. He died on Aug. 7, 1868.

Mexican general **Mariano Arista** was in command of Mexican troops in the battles of Palo Alto and Resaca de la Palma in the Mexican War. After losing both engagements to Gen. Zachary Taylor he relinquished command. He became the constitutional president of Mexico in 1851 and resigned in 1853. He died near Lisbon, Portugal, on Aug. 7, 1855.

Capt. **Henry Bainbridge** of the 3rd Infantry (later the 7th), whom Col. Hitchcock thought was "too fond of his comforts," was wounded in the battle of Monterrey and was killed in the burning of the steamer Louisiana in Galveston Bay on May 31, 1857.

Samuel Bangs, who began publishing the "Corpus Christi Gazette" on Jan. 1, 1846, followed the army to the Rio Grande and published the American Flag in Matamoros.

After the war, he operated a hotel at Port Isabel. He was captured by Indians while traveling by stage from Port Isabel to Brownsville and freed in "a state of nudity" with other passengers. He moved to Georgetown, Ky., where he died of typhoid fever in 1854.

Merchant **Frederick Belden** was engaged in the Mexican trade and became friends with Zachary Taylor during the army's stay in Corpus Christi. Belden died in 1867 and his widow Mauricia Arocha Belden in 1896. Belden Street in Corpus Christi was named in his honor.

Henry W. Berry married Elizabeth Moore, the young lady courted by Lt. Grant and other officers of the army. She died in childbirth two years later. Berry was elected sheriff in 1846 and became a builder and brick maker. He died on May 15, 1888 and was buried in Old Bayview Cemetery.

First Lt. **Jacob E. Blake**, of the Topographical Engineers, was killed at Palo Alto on May 9, 1846 by the discharge of his own pistol. "As he took his pistol off at night," wrote James Longstreet, "he threw it upon the ground, and an accidental explosion of one of the charges gave him a mortal wound."

Capt. **W. W. Bliss**, "Perfect Bliss," Gen. Taylor's adjutant who joked that Grant lost "five or six dollars' worth of horses," was brevetted major after the battles of Palo Alto and Resaca de la Palma then lieutenant colonel for his actions at Buena Vista. He died in 1853 in Pascagoula, Miss.

Sarah Bourjett, later Sarah Bowman, the madam laundress, opened a fancy "hotel" in El Paso after the Mexican War. Ranger Capt. Rip Ford saw her there and said she could whip any man, "fair fight or foul." She moved on to Fort Yuma, Ariz., where she married Albert Bowman and died from the bite of a tarantula spider on Dec. 23, 1866. The Army in 1890 exhumed the bodies at the Fort Yuma post cemetery and moved them to the presidio at San Francisco, which is now the last resting place of the Great Western.

First Lt. **Braxton Bragg** of the 3rd Artillery, whose slave was killed by lightning at Corpus Christi, was in the bombardment of Fort Brown and the battles of Buena Vista and Monterrey. In the Civil War, he was a lieutenant general in the Confederate Army. He died at Galveston in 1876. Fort Bragg, N. C., was named for him.

First Lt. **Forbes Britton**, quartermaster with the 7th Regiment at Corpus Christi, was in charge of the army's depot at Camargo. After the war, Britton returned to Corpus Christi, entered the mercantile trade, and was elected to the Texas Senate from Corpus Christi in 1857. He died in 1861.

Maj. **Jacob Brown** of the 7th Infantry was hit by a shell fragment during the bombardment of Fort Texas on May 6, 1846. He died three days later and was buried by the fort's flagstaff. The fort was renamed Fort Brown in his memory. The city of Brownsville grew up around its walls.

First Lt. **Daniel T. Chandler**, quartermaster of the 3rd Regiment, who planted the first American flag over Texas soil on St. Joseph's Island, was in battles in Mexico at Monterrey, Churubusco and Contreras, where he was wounded. He was a Confederate colonel in the Civil War; died in Baltimore, Md., in 1877.

Lt. Col. **Thomas Childs**, a veteran of the War of 1812, was in command of an artillery battalion at Palo Alto and

Resaca de la Palma. He died Oct. 8, 1853 at Fort Brooke, Fla.

Louis P. Cooke, citizen of Corpus Christi and suspect in the ambush of a Lipan chief, followed the army to Mexico in 1846 and opened a store in Matamoros and transported sutler's goods for the army to Monterrey. He died on March 3, 1849 in Brownsville.

Capt. **Thomas Cram**, of the Topographical Engineers, Lt. Meade's superior officer, suffered a bout of malaria at Corpus Christi and was sent North for his health before the battle of Palo Alto.

Col. **Trueman Cross**, assistant quartermaster general of the army, rode off from camp without an escort on the Rio Grande on April 10, 1846 and was killed by Mexican bandits. His body was found ten days later hidden in brush by the river. He was buried by the flagstaff in front of Fort Brown and later that year his body was moved to the Congressional Cemetery in Washington, D.C.

Lt. **Napoleon Jackson Tecumseh Dana**, of the 7th Infantry, whose brother-in-law was Capt. Daniel P. Whiting, was in the bombardment of Fort Brown and was wounded at the battle of Cerro Gordo, hit in the hip with a musket ball which proved to be a lingering injury. He was a major general in the Union Army during the Civil War. He died July 15, 1905.

Jose de Alba, editor of Samuel Bangs' "Corpus Christi Gazette" in 1846, was appointed chief justice of Nueces County when the county was organized in January 1847. His name disappeared from the local records soon afterwards.

Lt. **Edward Deas,** who exchanged shots in a duel with a sutler named Irwin in Corpus Christi, drowned in the Rio Grande on May 16, 1849.

Second Lt. **Abner Doubleday** of the 1st Artillery was a lieutenant with the 1st Artillery who found Corpus Christi a fine place "for those who dislike the restraints of civilization." He was in the battles of Buena Vista and Monterrey. He fired the Union guns in the defense of Fort Sumter at the start of the Civil War. He commanded I Corps of the Army of the Potomac after the death of John Reynolds at the battle of Gettysburg. He served in the occupation forces in Texas after the war. He died in 1893.

Lt. **Joseph H. Eaton**, Gen. Taylor's aide-de-camp, was a paymaster for the Union Army during the Civil War.

Ramon Falcon, a Mexican bandit (or guerrilla leader) who was blamed for ambushing and killing Col. Trueman Cross, was captured near Saltillo and hanged on Dec. 19, 1847.

Second Lt. **Samuel G. French,** in Ringgold's battery of horse artillery, was at Palo Alto and Resaca de la Palma. He resigned the army in 1856 and became a planter near Vicksburg. He was a major general in the Confederate Army in the Civil War.

Second Lt. **Levi Gantt**, of the 7th Infantry, was killed on Sept.13, 1847 at the battle of Chapultepec.

Capt. **Richard Gatlin**, of the 7th, was wounded at the battle of Monterrey. He was a brigadier general in the Confederate Army in the Civil War.

Second Lt. **Ulysses S. Grant** of the 4th Regiment, in his eagerness to disembark, fell into Corpus Christi Bay when he arrived. Grant, who was nicknamed "Beauty" for his good looks, was cast as "Desdemona" in a play but was dropped because the male actor couldn't summon up enough passion to kiss him in a scene. In the Civil War, he was promoted to lieutenant general and commander in chief of the Union Army in March 1864. He accepted Lee's surrender at Appomattox. He was elected president in 1869 and served two terms. He spent his last year writing his memoirs, which he completed four days before he died of throat cancer, on July 23, 1885.

Capt. **Mabry B. Gray**, called "Mustang," led a company of Texas Mounted Volunteers that was sent back from northern Mexico to protect Corpus Christi in the fall of 1846. It had been rumored, falsely as it turned out, that Comanches had attacked and decimated the town. After Gray's company of "Mustangers" was ordered back to Camargo they were accused of committing atrocities at Rancho Guadalupe, a village where 24 civilians were massacred (avenging the massacre of Patterson Rogers' supply train).. Gray died in Camargo in February 1848.

Capt. **William J. Hardee**, of the 2nd Dragoons, who was captured near Matamoros before the battle of Palo Alto, became a Confederate general during the Civil War.

Brevet Maj. **Edgar S. Hawkins**, who took command of Fort Brown during the bombardment after Major Jacob Brown was killed, Nov. 5, 1865 at Flatbush, N. Y.

Surgeon **Hamilton S. Hawkins**, whose wife joined him at the encampment at Corpus Christi, died Aug. 7, 1847 in Mexico.

First Lt. **Alexander Hays**, 4th Regiment, was in the battles of Palo Alto and Resaca de la Palma. He was a brigadier general in the Union Army in the Civil War, killed on May 5, 1864 at the battle of the Wilderness.

Col. **John Coffee Hays**, famed Texas Ranger captain, commanded a regiment of Texas volunteers that fought with Zachary Taylor's army at Monterrey. He formed another regiment the following year that helped keep Winfield Scott's supply lines open between Veracruz and Mexico City. He moved to California after the war, was elected sheriff of San Francisco and helped found the city of Oakland. He died in 1883.

First Lt. **W. S. Henry** (William Seton) of the 3rd Regiment, who ate "themales" at Mrs. Belden's in Corpus Christi and was among the last to leave when the army marched off to the Rio Grande, fought at Palo Alto, Resaca de la Palma, Monterrey and Buena Vista. He wrote "Campaign Sketches of the War with Mexico." He died at age 34 at West Point on March 5, 1851 and was buried in the Post Cemetery.

Lt. Col. **Ethan Allen Hitchcock**, commander of the 3rd Regiment, who spent his time at Corpus Christi in his tent with diarrhea and Spinoza, served as an adviser to Gen. Winfield Scott and was put in charge of covert operations during the war in Mexico. In the Civil War, he acted as a military adviser to Abraham Lincoln. He died in Sparta, Ga., on Aug. 4, 1870.

Surgeon **N. S. Jarvis**, of the General Staff, who was in charge of the army's general hospital during the Corpus Christi encampment, died on May 12, 1862 during the Civil War while he was medical director of the Department of Maryland.

Capt. **Croghan Ker**, of the 2nd Dragoons, involved in a court-martial at Corpus Christi for a "disgraceful brawl over a low woman," was in the battle of Palo Alto and severely wounded at Molino del Rey.

Henry Kinney, the founder of Corpus Christi whose lobbying efforts brought Gen. Zachary Taylor and half the U.S. Army to Corpus Christi in the summer of 1845, was appointed to the staff of James Pinckney Henderson, in command of Texas troops, and served as a quartermaster with the rank of major. He led a philibustering expedition to Nicaragua in 1855. Kinney was shot to death outside the home of his former lover in Matamoros, Mexico in February 1862.

Second Lt. **James Longstreet** of the 4th Regiment, one of the leaders behind building the Army Theater at Corpus Christi, was in battles at Contreras, Churubusco, and Molino del Rey. He was wounded at Chapultepec. He was a lieutenant general in Lee's Army of Northern Virginia in the Civil War. He died in Gainesville, Ga., in 1904.

Capt. **Allen Lowd**, of the 2nd Artillery, in charge of a battery of 24-pounder guns during the bombardment of Fort Brown, was promoted to brevet major after the battle. He died July 9, 1853 at New Holland, Pa.

Capt. **George A. McCall**, 4th Infantry, was later an assistant adjutant general. In the Civil War he commanded the Pennsylvania Reserve in the federal Army of the Potomac.

Lt. Col. **James S. McIntosh**, known as "Old Tosh," was commander of the 2nd Brigade at Corpus Christi (5th and 7th regiments of infantry) had a bayonet thrust through his mouth and neck at Resaca de la Palama. He died Sept. 26, 1847 of wounds received in the battle of Molino del Rey.

Second Lt. **Lafayette McLaws** of the 7th Infantry, shot in an accident in San Antonio in 1845, was in the defense of Fort Brown and the siege of Vera Cruz. He was a major general in the Confederate Army during the Civil War and commanded a division of Lee's army in the battle of Gettysburg.

First Lt. **John B. (Bankhead) Magruder** was in the 1st Artillery at Corpus Christi, where he joined James Longstreet as one of the principal organizers of the Union Theater. In the Civil War, Magruder, who was called "Prince John," was a major general with Lee's Army of Northern Virginia until he was transferred to Texas in October 1862. He was in command when Galveston was recaptured on Jan. 1, 1863.

Bvt. Major **Joseph K. F. Mansfield**, of the engineer corps, who designed Fort Brown and oversaw its construction, was in the bombardment of the fort and the battle of Monterrey, in which he was severely wounded. He was a Union general during the Civil War; he died of wounds received at Antietam on Sept. 18, 1862.

Sgt. Major **Charles Masland** of the 3rd Infantry, who wrote letters to his brother and other family members in Massachusetts, was killed in the battle of Resaca de la Palma.

Capt. **Charles A. May**, 2nd Regiment of Dragoons, was in the battles of Palo Alto, Resaca de la Palma and Buena Vista. He died on Dec. 24, 1864.

Second Lt. **George Gordon Meade** of the Topographical Engineers made exploratory trips up the Nueces River, the Laguna Madre, and inner bays. He is credited with making the first accurate maps of the lower Nueces River, the

Laguna Madre, and the inner bays. He was in the battles of Palo Alto, Resaca de la Palma and Monterrey. In the Civil War, he was appointed commander of the Army of the Potomac shortly before the battle of Gettysburg. He died at his home in Philadelphia on Nov. 6, 1872.

Second Lt. **John James Peck**, of the Light Artillery, fought at Palo Alto, Resaca de la Palma and other battles in the Mexican War. He was a major general in the Union Army during the Civil War. He died in Syracuse, N.Y., in 1878.

Lt. **Theodoric Porter,** whose acting ability did not extend to being able to kiss U.S. Grant as Desdemona, was killed on April 19 while he was out searching for Col. Truman Cross, quartermaster general of Taylor's headquarters staff, across the river from Matamoros. The body of Cross was found three days later. Porter was the son of Navy Commodore David Dixon Porter.

First Lt. **Owen P. Ransom** of the 2nd Dragoons, involved in a brawl with Capt. Ker at Corpus Christi, was discharged from the service following a court martial.

Lt. **Isaac Reeve** of the 8th Regiment, severely injured when he was kicked by a horse at Corpus Christi, recovered and went on to fight in several battles in the Mexican War and later was a Union colonel in the Civil War.

Second Lt. **John F. (Fulton) Reynolds** was with the 3rd Artillery at Corpus Christi. He was brevetted captain then major following the battles of Monterrey and Buena Vista. Reynolds became a major general in the Civil War and was offered command of the Army of the Potomac, but he made conditions Lincoln would not accept. His friend George Meade got the command instead. Reynolds, in command of I Corps, was killed in the first day's clash at Gettysburg, the highest-ranking officer on either side killed in the battle.

Lt. **John A. Richey** of the 4th Infantry, who was at the battles of Palo Alto and Resaca de la Palma, was killed by Mexican guerrillas at Villa Grande on Jan. 13, 1847.

First Lt. **Randolph Ridgely** of the 3rd Artillery, whose game of brag at Corpus Christi led to a duel, was at Palo Alto and Resaca de la Palma. He died Oct. 27, 1846 at Monterrey when his horse fell, dashing his head on the pavement. Grant, who attended Ridgely's funeral, said he had been a great young gunner and that he, along with Duncan and Braxton Bragg, did much to win the battles at Palo Alto and Resaca de la Palma.

Brevet Major **Samuel Ringgold** of the 3rd Artillery died May 11, 1846 from wounds received in the battle of Palo Alto.

Lt. **Jeremiah M. Scarritt** of the Engineers, who cut a gap in the reef across Nueces Bay, was promoted to brevet captain after the battle of Monterrey. He died at Key West, Fla., on June 22, 1854.

Lt. **E. (Ephraim) Kirby Smith**, of the 5th Regiment, whose letters to his wife were quoted here, was killed at the battle of Molina del Rey. His younger brother Edmund was also with the army.

Lt. **E. (Edmund) Kirby Smith**, was initially in the 5th Regiment and afterwards in the 7th Infantry Regiment, later became the well-known Confederate general.

Brigadier Gen. **Zachary Taylor**, commander of the "Army of Occupation" at Corpus Christi in late 1845 and early

1846, commander in the field at the battles of Palo Alto, Resaca de la Palma, Monterrey and Buena Vista, died on July 9, 1850, in the White House while President of the United States. His last words were "I regret nothing, but am sorry that I am about to leave my friends." It was Tuesday night, July 9, 1850.

Second Lt. **George H. Thomas** was in Braxton Bragg's company of the 3rd Artillery. In the Civil War, he refused to join the Confederacy and his Virginia family cut all ties with him. As commander of the Army of the Cumberland he was called the "Rock of Chickamauga" for his steadfast courage. He annihilated John B. Hood's army at Nashville. Military historians consider him one of the ablest generals in the Union Army. Besides Thomas, the 3rd Artillery at Corpus Christi produced four other Civil War generals: Braxton Bragg, John F. Reynolds, John J. Peck, and Samuel G. French.

Capt. **Seth B. Thornton**, of the 2nd Dragoons, who was captured by Mexican forces a week before the battle of Palo Alto, was killed Aug. 18, 1847 in Mexico.

Josiah Turner, who came to Corpus Christi to look for work in the winter of 1845, described the town for the Corpus Christi Weekly Caller, printed in the Jan. 24, 1904 edition. He was a visitor in the city from the Galveston Ranch in Cameron County.

Col. **David E. Twiggs**, commander of the 2nd Dragoons at Corpus Christi, was promoted to brigadier general after Palo Alto and Resaca de la Palma and brevetted a major general after the battle at Monterrey. He commanded the U.S. Army's Department of Texas at the beginning of the Civil War and was vilified in the north for surrendering Texas military forts without a struggle. He was later commissioned a major general in the Confederate Army. He died on July 15, 1862 in Georgia.

Lt. **Earl Van Dorn** of the 7th Infantry raised the American flag during the bombardment of Fort Brown. He was in the battles of Cerro Gordo, Contreras and Churubusco, where he was wounded. In the Civil War, he was a major general in the Confederate Army. On May 7, 1863, Van Dorn was shot and killed (most accounts say "assassinated") in his office in Spring Hill, Tenn. He was shot by a doctor who claimed Van Dorn, known for his drinking and womanizing, had violated "the sanctity of his marriage."

Col. **William Whistler** of the 4th Infantry and commander of the 3rd Brigade at Corpus Christi, of whom Hitchcock said he couldn't form his troops into line, retired from the army in 1861 and died on Dec. 4, 1863.

Capt. **Daniel P. Whiting**, of the 7th Regiment, who sketched a bird's-eye view of the encampment of Corpus Christi and other scenes of the campaign in Mexico, was in the bombardment of Fort Brown, the battle of Monterrey, siege of Vera Cruz, and battle of Cerro Gordo. After the Mexican War he took part in the Utah expedition in 1858. In the Civil War he was promoted to lieutenant colonel but ill health kept him from the field. He died on Aug. 2, 1892 at the age of 84.

Col. **William J. Worth,** described as the Marshal Ney of the Army, was in the battle of Monterrey and led the first troops ashore at Veracruz and commanded the troops that captured Chapultepec Castle in Mexico City. He was promoted to brevet major general. After the war, Worth commanded the Department of Texas and died during a cholera outbreak in San Antonio in 1849. The city of Fort Worth was named in his honor.

APPENDIX 2

List of Officers

List of army officers that were encamped at Corpus Christi from Aug. 1, 1845 to March 12, 1846:

GENERAL STAFF

Brigadier General Zachary Taylor, Commanding. Captain W. W. S. Bliss assistant adjutant general. First Lt J. H. Eaton, 3rd infantry aide-de-camp. Lt. Col. M. M. Payne, 4th artillery, inspector general, "army of occupation."

Colonel T. Cross, assistant quartermaster general. Major C. Thomas, quartermaster, (St. Joseph's). Major S. McRee, quartermaster, (St. Joseph's.) Captain G. H. Crosman, assistant quartermaster, Captain E. S. Sibley, assistant quartermaster, Captain E. A. Ogden, assistant quartermaster, Captain W. S. Ketchum, assistant quartermaster, Captain G. G. Waggaman, commissary of subsistence.

Surgeon P. H. Craig, medical director. Surgeon N. S. Jarvis. Assistant Surgeon B. M. Byrne, (St. Joseph's). Assistant Surgeon J. R. Conrad. Paymaster St. Clair Denny. Paymaster Lloyd J. Beall. Paymaster Roger S. Dix.

ENGINEERS

Captain J. K. Mansfield. Captain John Sanders. First Lt. J. M. Scarritt.

TOPOGRAPHICAL ENGINEERS
Captain Thomas Cram, First Lt. J. E. Blake. Second Lt. George Meade.

ORDNANCE DEPARTMENT
Captain G. D, Ramsay. Second Lt. C. P. Kingsbury, (St. Joseph's.)

LIGHT ARTILLERY
Major John Erving, 2nd artillery. Assistant Surgeon J. B. Wells, general staff. Second Lt. S. Fahnestock, 4th artillery, acting adjutant. *Brevet Majors:* John Munroe, 4th artillery. Samuel Ringgold, 3rd artillery.
First lieutenants: James Duncan, 2nd artillery. Braxton Bragg, 3rd artillery; J. F. Roland, 2nd artillery, Randolph Ridgely, 3rd artillery. W. H. Shover, 3rd artillery. E. Bradford, 4th artillery. J. C. Pemberton, 4th artillery. G. H. Thomas, 3rd artillery. *Second lieutenants:* William Hays, 2nd artillery. John F. Reynolds, 3rd artillery. John J. Peck, 2nd artillery. S. L. Fremont, 3rd artillery. M. Lovell, 4th artillery. J. P. Johnstone, 4th artillery. Samuel G, French, 3rd artillery.

SECOND REGIMENT OF DRAGOONS
Colonel David E. Twiggs, commanding. Assistant Surgeon L. C. McPhail, general staff. First Lt. H. H. Sibley, adjutant. *Captains:* Croghan Ker, Charles A. May, Seth B. Thornton, W. J. Hardee. *First Lieutenants:* W. H. Saunders, F. Hamilton, A. Lowry, O. F. Winship. *Second Lieutenants:* R. P. Campbell, George Stevens, R. H. Anderson, W. Steele, Lewis Neill, G. T. Mason, D. B. Sackett.

FIRST BRIGADE
Brevet Brigadier General William J. Worth, commanding. First Lt. Larkin Smith, 8th infantry, aide de

camp. Surgeon H. S. Hawkins, general staff. Surgeon J. J. B. Wright, general staff. Assistant surgeon D. C. DeLeon, general staff.

BATTALION OF ARTILLERY

Brevet Lt. Col. Thomas Childs, commanding. Second Lt. R. S. Garnett, 4th artillery, acting adjutant. *Brevet Majors:* J. Dimick, 1st artillery. W. W. Morris, 4th artillery. *Captains.* Giles Porter, 1st artillery. Martin Burke, 3rd artillery. A. Lowd, 2nd artillery. C. F. Smith, 2nd artillery. J. B. Scott, 4th artillery. R. C. Smead, 4th artillery.

First lieutenants: M. Knowlton, 1st artillery. E. Deas, 4th artillery. R. A. Luther, 2nd artillery. G. Taylor, 3rd artillery. Arnold Elzey, 2nd artillery. W. H. Churchill. 3rd artillery. John B. Magruder, 1st artillery. J. S. Hatheway, 1st artillery. C. B. Daniels, 2nd artillery. W. H. Fowler, 1st artillery. W. Gilham, 3rd artillery. J. P. McCown, 4th artillery.

Second Lieutenants: L. Chase, 2nd artillery. A. B. Lansing, 2nd artillery. A. A. Gibson, 2nd artillery. W. S. Smith, 1st artillery. S. K. Dawson, 1st artillery. J. F. Irons, 1st artillery. H. M. Whiting, 4th artillery. S. Williams, 1st artillery. H. F. Clarke, 2nd artillery. S. Gill 4th artillery. J. F. Farry, 4th artillery. George W. Ayres, 3rd artillery. C. Benjamin, 4th artillery. C. L. Kilburn, 3rd artillery. Abner Doubleday, 3rd artillery. J. J. Reynolds, 4th artillery. T. J, Curd 1st artillery. Thomas B. J. Weld, 1st artillery.

8TH REGIMENT OF INFANTRY

Brevet Lieutenant Colonel W. G. Belknap, commanding. Second Lt. John D. Clark, acting adjutant. *Captains:* W. R. Montgomery, W. O. Kello, R. B. Screven, H. McKavett, J. V. Bomford. *First Lieutenants:* J. V. D. Reeve, G. Lincoln, J. Selden, C. R. Gates, A. L. Sheppard, A. T. Lee. *Second Lieutenants:* R. P. Maclay, J. Beardsley, C. D. Jordan, T. L. Chadbourne, E. B. Holloway, C. G. Merchant, T. J.

Montgomery, J. G. Burbank, C. F. Morris, J. J. Booker, James Longstreet, H. M. Judah, George Wainwright, J. G. S. Snelling.

SECOND BRIGADE

Lieutenant Colonel J. S. McIntosh, 5th infantry, commanding. Ist Lt. C. L. Stevenson, 5th infantry, Brigade Major. Surgeon R. C. Wood, general staff. Assistant Surgeon J. W. Russell, general staff. H. E. Crittenden, general staff.

5TH REGIMENT OF INFANTRY

Major T. Staniford, commanding, First Lt. G. Deas, adjutant. *Captains:* Martin Scott, M. E. Merrill, A. Drane, E. K. Smith, A. S. Hooe, C. C. Sibley, J. L. Thompson, W. Chapman. *First Lieutenants:* R. B. Marcy, J. H. Whipple, N. B. Rossell, D. Ruggles, W. Root, J. A. Whitall. *Second Lieutenants:* S. H. Fowler, S. Norvell, H. Whiting, M. Rosecrants, T. G Pitcher, R. L. Brooke, J. C. Robinson, P. Lugenbeel, J. P. Smith, W. L. Crittenden.

7TH REGIMENT OF INFANTRY

Major Jacob Brown, commanding. Second Lt. F. N. Page, adjutant. *Captains:* E. S. Hawkins, D. S. Miles, J. G. Rains, T. Holmes, Daniel P. Whiting, F. Lee, W. Seawell, S. W. Moore, R. H. Ross, R. C. Gatlin. *First Lieutenants:* Forbes Britton, N. Hopson, J. B. Scott, A. Montgomery, C. Hanson, C. H. Humber. *Second Lieutenants.* L. Gantt, Earl Van Dorn, J. H. Potter, A Crozet, J. M. Henry, S. B. Hayman, F. Gardner, W. K. Van Bokkelen, E. B. Strong, H. B. Clitz, and W. H. Wood.

THIRD BRIGADE

Colonel W. Whistler, 4th infantry, brigade major. Assistant Surgeon J. B. Porter, general staff. Assistant

Surgeon M. Mills, general staff. Assistant Surgeon J. Simons, general staff. A. W. Kennedy, general staff.

THIRD REGIMENT OF INFANTRY

Lieutenant Colonel Ethan Allen Hitchcock, commanding. First Lt. F. D. S. Irwin, adjutant. *Captains:* L. N. Norris, J. Van Horne, G. P. Field, H. Bainbridge, J. L. Colburn. *First Lieutenants:* P. N. Barbour, L. S. Craig, W. H. Gordon, W. S. Henry, J. M. Smith, D. T. Chandler, O. L. Shepherd. *Second Lieutenants:* W. B. Johns, D. C. Buell, W. T. H. Brooks, A. J. Williamson, J. C. McFerran, J. J. C. Bibb, Thomas Jordan, I. B. Richardson, A. W. Bowman, R. Hazlitt, G. C. McClelland, J. P. Hatch, B. E. Bee.

FOURTH REGIMENT OF INFANTRY

Lieutenant Colonel J. Garland, commanding. First Lieutenant C. Hoskins, adjutant. Brevet Major G. W. Allen, acting major.

Captains: John Page, P. Morrison, G. Morris, W. M. Graham, George A. McCall, R. C. Buchanan, C. H. Larnard. *First Lieutenants:* B. Alvord, R. E. Cochrane, Richard H. Graham, E. G. Elliott. *Second Lieutenants:* T. H. Porter, H. D. Wallen, C. C. Augur, J. S. Woods, Sidney Smith, J. Beaman, U. S. Grant, J. A. Richey, P. A. Farelly.

—*Corpus Christi Gazette, Jan. 22. 1846*

List of Deaths

Soldiers with Zachary Taylor's army who died during the seven-month encampment at Corpus Christi:

Lt. William T. Allen, 2nd Dragoons. Pvt. Archibald Blalock, 4th Infantry. Sgt. Joseph Butcher, 4th Artillery. Pvt. Samuel Byars, 3rd Artillery.

Pvt. Lawrence Callahan, 2nd Artillery. Pvt. David R. Camp, 3rd Infantry. Pvt. James Cashman, 2nd Artillery. Pvt. John Clark, 2nd Dragoons. Pvt. Robert Coe, 2nd Artillery. Lt. Augustus Cook, 2nd Dragoons.

Jeremiah Denton, a musician with the 7th Infantry. Pvt. Jacob Druves, 3rd Artillery. Pvt. Jacob T. Edgar, 2nd Dragoons. Pvt. John Eisenberger, 3rd Infantry. —— Engenspiehl (no unit listed).

Cpl. John Ford, 5th Infantry. Cpl. Elza B. Forrest, 3rd Infantry. Cpl. William Forrey, 3rd Infantry. Pvt. Daniel H. Fowler, 4th Infantry. Pvt. Patrick Foy, 2nd Dragoons. Pvt. William Fraser, 7th Infantry.

Pvt. Robert Galloway, 4th Infantry. Pvt. William Garey, 2nd Dragoons. Pvt. George Gettner, 3rd Artillery. Pvt. James Goodhand, 5th Infantry. Pvt. William Graham, 8th Infantry.

Lt. James O. Handy, 8th Infantry. Pvt. Ardel Hearty, 3rd Infantry. Pvt. Francis Hellan, 2nd Dragoons. Pvt. Henry Henerman, 3rd Infantry. Pvt. Reuben Herbert, 3rd Infantry. Lt. Col. William Hoffman, 7th Infantry. Pvt. Hugh Hogan,

2nd Artillery. Pvt. Peter Hughs, 3rd Infantry. Cpl. Alfred Humphries, 8th Infantry.

Pvt. William Jeffries, 5th Infantry. Pvt. Ludwig Kaisen, 4th Infantry. Pvt. Edward Kelly, 2nd Dragoons. Pvt. Joseph Kelly, 2nd Dragoons. Pvt. Thomas Kennedy, 3rd Infantry. Pvt. John Lewars, 4th Infantry. Pvt. John Lugenbuhl, 7th Infantry.

Pvt. John F. Marcellis, 2nd Dragoons. Pvt. John Martin, 3rd Infantry. Sgt. Edward McCall, 5th Infantry. Pvt. John McLowlen, 4th Infantry. Lt. Henry Merrill, 5th Infantry. Pvt. Henry Messersmith, 5th Infantry. Pvt. David Miller, 3rd Infantry. Pvt. John F. Miller, 4th Artillery. Pvt. William W. Mills, 4th Infantry. Pvt. John Monghan, 4th Infantry. Pvt. Patrick Murphy, 8th Infantry. Pvt. Robert Murphy, 4th Infantry.

Pvt. John M. Pugh, 8th Infantry. Pvt. Andrew Reifstack, 2nd Dragoons. Pvt. John F. B. Richardson, 4th Infantry. Sgt. James Riddle, 2nd Artillery. Pvt. Michael Sanders, 4th Infantry. Pvt. Elijah W. Staton, 3rd Infantry. Pvt. Robert Stewart, 4th Infantry. Pvt. Gutlieb van Allmen, 4th Infantry. Pvt. William W. Wade, 5th Infantry. Sgt. Ulysses W. Warner, 2nd Dragoons. Capt. ——West (no unit listed). Pvt. Joseph Wilson, 8th Infantry. Pvt. Camile Young, 2nd Dragoons. And others unknown.

Killed in the steamboat Dayton explosion, Sept. 12, 1845:

Lt. Benjamin A. Berry, 4th Infantry. Cpl. ——Chambers (no unit listed). Sgt. Richard Edwards, 3rd Infantry. Lt. Thaddeus Higgins, 4th Infantry. Pvt. John Hughes, 3rd Infantry. Pvt. Alexander Iwanowski, 2nd Dragoons. Pvt. James Johnson, 3rd Infantry. Pvt. James Marshall, 4th Infantry. Sgt. Daniel McKerns, 3rd Infantry.

—Old Bayview Cemetery

APPENDIX 4

Chronology

June 19, 1845
Zachary Taylor received orders from Washington to move his command from Fort Jesup to Texas.

July 7
The 3rd Infantry Regiment, under Col. Hitchcock, left Fort Jesup and traveled by steamboat to New Orleans.

July 10
The 3rd Infantry arrived in New Orleans.

July 17
The 2nd Dragoons departed Fort Jesup on an overland march to join Taylor in Texas.

July 23
The 3rd Infantry and Taylor's staff embarked on the steamboat Alabama for Texas.

July 25
Steamboat Alabama arrived at Aransas Pass near sundown.

July 26
The U.S. flag planted on a sand dune on St. Joseph's Island.

July 31
First companies of 3rd Infantry land on North Beach.

Aug. 1
Work to clear ground on the shoreline for a camp got underway.

Aug. 14
The schooner Swallow loaded with supplies wrecked trying to cross the bar. A wreck sale was held a week later.

Aug. 15

Gen. Taylor and his staff landed at Corpus Christi from St. Joseph's.

Aug. 21

Henry Kinney returned to Corpus Christi from Austin, along with his escort of Lipan warriors.

Aug. 23

The 2nd Dragoons reached San Patricio after their overland march from Fort Jesup.

Aug. 24

Severe thunderstorm hit the encampment. Braxton Bragg's slave killed by a lightning bolt.

Aug. 28

First companies of the 7th Infantry land and set up camp.

Sept. 3

Man arrested trying to encourage a slave to escape.

Sept. 7

Hitchcock on a visit to Henry Kinney's home met Kinney's friend and spy, Chipito Sandoval, who would keep Taylor informed of troop movements and political developments in Mexico.

Sept. 12

Boilers on the steamboat Dayton, a lighter hired to carry troops from St. Joseph's, explode. The men killed in the accident were buried in a cemetery that would later be called Old Bayview.

Sept. 18

Scouting expedition left to travel up the Nueces River.

October

Soldiers were detailed to work clearing a flat tableland a mile west of the camp, on the bluff, for drills and maneuvers.

Oct. 13

The steamer Alabama arrived with five companies of the 5th Infantry, the last of the troops assigned to Taylor's command at Corpus Christi.

Oct. 23

A group of officers on a hunting trip up the Nueces River killed deer, geese and a seven-foot panther.

Nov. 3

Full-dress review of the 2nd Dragoons was followed by a review of the Louisiana Volunteer Artillery, shortly before that unit's departure for home the next day.

Nov. 18

Lt. Cook of the 2nd Dragoons killed himself by jumping overboard on the way to Galveston.

Nov. 20

A cold norther brought rain and misery.

Nov. 25

Lt. George Meade returned with topographical engineers from an exploration of the Laguna Madre.

Nov. 26

Lt. Col. William Hoffman died.

Nov. 30

Norther brought Arctic-like temperatures.

Dec. 3

Cold weather continues. Temperature dropped to 23 degrees; cartloads of fish stranded along the shore.

December.

U.S. Grant, other officers, for a diversion, accompanied a paymaster's wagon train to San Antonio.

Dec. 11

Charles G. Bryant's Union Theater opened.

Dec. 12

Quarrel over brevet rank roiled the camp. Hitchcock composed a "memorial" to send to Congress, signed by most of the officers at Corpus Christi.

Jan. 1, 1846

Taylor celebrated New Year's by sharing egg nog with the officers in his command. The first edition of the Corpus Christi Gazette was published.

Jan. 8

Army Theater opened with a play called "The Wife." Duel was fought between a lieutenant and a storekeeper.

Jan. 21

Lt Meade and other topographical engineers depart on an expedition to explore and map the inner bays, from Corpus Christi Bay to Matagorda Bay.

February

Taylor received orders to move the army to the Rio Grande.

Feb. 8

Rev. John Hayne, a Methodist minister, preached a sermon at the Union Theater.

Feb. 16

Corpus Christi celebrated the emergence of the state of Texas and the end of the Republic with an "Annexation Ball."

February

Camp stayed busy with preparations for departure. Surrounding country was scoured for wagons, carts, oxen, horses and mules.

Feb. 21

Two reconnaissance parties sent to find a suitable route of march to the border returned.

March 4

Squad dispatched to establish a supply depot on Santa Gertrudis Creek as the army prepared to march south. The 2nd dragoons visited the quartermaster to have their sabers and knives sharpened. Order of march published in the Corpus Christi Gazette.

March 8

The 2nd Dragoons and a company of artillery marched out of Corpus Christi at 10 in the morning.

March 9

The 1st Brigade, composed of the 8th Infantry regiment and the 4th Artillery, marched south. -

March 10

The 2nd Brigade, composed of the 5th and 7th regiments, departed.

March 11

The 3rd Brigade, with Taylor's staff, the 3rd artillery, and the 3rd and 4th regiments of infantry, was the last to leave.

March 11-17
   Taylor's regiments struggle to cross the bleak, Sahara-like
   sand belt called "The Sands" or the Desert of the Dead.
March 18
   Lead elements of Taylor's four columns approached the
   Arroyo Colorado. Taylor decided to halt and re-concentrate
   the army regiments before crossing.
March 20-22
   Regiments crossed the Arroyo Colorado. Threatened Mexican
   resistance melted away.
March 23
   Taylor's four columns began the march in the direction of
   Matamoros, 28 miles away.
March 28
   American flag was raised on the left bank of the Rio Grande
   as the regimental bands played "Yankee Doodle."
April 3
   Work began on a gun battery for four 18-pounders that would
   bear directly on Matamoros.
April 5
   Ground was broken behind the battery for a fortified
   enclosure of six bastions capable of holding up to 2,000 men.
   It was originally called "Fort Texas" and later renamed "Fort
   Brown."
April 8
   A norther with heavy rain hit the camp in a cornfield by the
   river. Tents were blown down, contents scattered, cooking
   fires drenched.
April 10
   Col. Trueman Cross, deputy quartermaster general, left camp
   for a morning ride and disappeared. Search parties found no
   trace of him.
April 11
   With a parade and ringing of church bells, Gen. Pedro de
   Ampudia rode into Matamoros to take command. He was
   soon relieved in favor of Gen. Mariano Arista.
April 12
   Col. Ethan A. Hitchcock of the 3rd Regiment was granted sick
   leave and departed from Point Isabel for New Orleans.

April 21
    The body of Col. Trueman Cross was found in a thicket by
    the river. He had been shot in the head, was stripped of his
    clothing, and his body mutilated by vultures.
April 24
    Col. Cross was buried at the foot of the flagpole in front of
    Fort Texas. In November, his body was disinterred and
    moved to Washington.
    A reconnaissance party led by Capts. Seth Thornton and
    William Hardee was ambushed at a hacienda 20 miles north
    of the fort. Seven men were killed and 46 captured, including
    Thornton and Hardee.
May 1
    Taylor assigned the 7th Infantry, along with artillery units, to
    garrison the fort while the remainder of the army marched
    toward Point Isabel to procure supplies and ammunition.
May 3
    Mexican batteries across the river began to fire on Fort Texas.
    Taylor's column at Point Isabel could hear the sounds of the
    cannon fire from 27 miles away.
May 4-6
    Bombardment of the fort continued.
May 6
    Maj. Jacob Brown was struck by a shell fragment and
    mortally wounded. He was buried by the flagpole three days
    later.
May 6-7
    Gen. Arista's forces crossed the river and took a position to
    block Taylor's return from Point Isabel.
May 8
    Taylor's forces came in sight of Arista's cavalry at a place
    called Palo Alto, where the first battle of the Mexican War
    was fought. After the battle, Arista retreated and Taylor
    followed.
May 9
    Arista and Taylor renewed the battle the next day at an old
    river channel called Resaca de la Palma. The ranks of the
    Mexican Army broke and fled along the river at full run.
    Taylor's victories at Palo Alto and Resaca de la Palma were

scored against a Mexican army three times the size of Taylor's own.

May 18

Taylor occupied Matamoros after Arista pulled out, leaving behind his sick and wounded. As Twiggs' dragoons crossed the Rio Grande, a regimental band played "Yankee Doodle."

APPENDIX 5

Billy's Mark

At the start of the Mexican War, William Rogers survived a terrible ordeal near the Rio Grande. In later years, fantastic stuff was said about "Billy" Rogers and part of it may be true.

William Long "Billy" Rogers was born in Alabama in 1822, one of 10 children of Patterson and Elizabeth Rogers. Patterson fought in the Seminole Wars in Florida, where he was a friend of Zachary Taylor, then he ran a hotel at Fort Jesup, La. His son-in-law, Roswell Denton, was appointed sutler (a storekeeper who sold goods on a military post).

When Taylor brought half the U.S. Army to Corpus Christi in 1845, the Rogers family followed. As the army moved to the Rio Grande in March 1846, a supply depot was established at Point Isabel. Taylor authorized Roswell Denton to forward army supplies. Denton prepared a wagon train to carry supplies to Point Isabel, under the supervision of Patterson and two sons, Anderson and Billy. Once on the border, Patterson planned to open a hotel to cater to the army.

Denton, in New Orleans to buy goods, wrote to warn his father-in-law that it was too dangerous to move a wagon train to the border without an army escort. There were too many bandits and guerrillas operating on the Rio Grande. The warning came too late.

The supply train left Corpus Christi on April 25, 1846, two weeks before the first battles of the Mexican War were fought at Palo Alto and Resaca de la Palma. Besides Patterson Rogers and two sons, members of the supply train were teamsters, with three women and four children.

The wagon train followed the trail left by Taylor's army and arrived at the Paso Real on the Arroyo Colorado on May 6, 1846.

Four miles south, they were surrounded by 50 or more guerrillas. Patterson Rogers and the teamsters, taken by surprise, surrendered and were forced to head back to the arroyo.

Two teamsters named Horton and Allenbrook were shot to death and a Mrs. Atwater was killed with a saber thrust. At the arroyo, 19 others were bound and stripped of their clothes; the bandits wanted the clothes without bloodstains. The women were raped. The throats of men, women and children were slashed and their bodies toppled into the river below. All were killed except one.

William Rogers missed death by an inch of a knife's blade. A deep gash severed his windpipe, but the blade missed his jugular. He was alive when pushed into the river. The bandits left him semi-conscious, without food, boots and clothing.

He was discovered nearly dead among the naked bodies of the Rogers party by Miguel Tijerina and three retainers; Jose Ma. Menchaca, Juan Arocha and Patricio Ramirez on the evening of May 7. After a journey toward Matamoras, the party encountered Don Domigo Guerra, Adolphus Glaevecke and several others traveling to see the battle site of Palo Alto. Guerra ordered Glaevecke to take Rogers into Matamoras for medical attention. Glaevecke, who had previously broken his parole in Matamoras, could not enter the city and took Rogers to Mrs. Brennan, an old American woman who lived on the Mexican side of the Rio Grande.

When the U.S. Army took possession of Matamoras, Rogers was turned over to the Army for further care by Army surgeon N. S. Garvis. Rogers recovered and rented a room in the home of Juan Corona. He later married Corona's daughter Julia.

War correspondent George Wilkins Kendall passed the site of the massacre. "We saw the remains of no less than seven of the unfortunate Rogers party, so cruelly murdered here a few weeks since," Kendall wrote. "Five skeletons, one of them apparently a female, were lying upon the banks, where they drifted after their throats had been cut; two others were discovered near the wagons. The wolves and buzzards had done their work."

After the war was over Rogers became a successful sheep rancher. He became a prominent man in Corpus Christi. He bought a ranch, was elected sheriff of Nueces County, then county judge, and sent to the Legislature. Rogers bought the St. James Hotel and he was a co-owner of Market Hall. In 1871, after his home burned, he organized Corpus Christi's first volunteer fire department and was its first President.

Rogers was a well-known citizen. What was not well-known, but whispered about, was that he once prowled the border searching for the bandits who killed his father and brother and left him for dead.

A few names of the bandits were known. The leader was one Juan Balli, also spelled as Juan Baillie. The plunder taken from the wagon train showed up in Reynosa. "Mustang" Gray's Rangers discovered that the Patterson Rogers killers were on a ranch near Matamoros. Gray's Rangers attacked the ranch and killed two dozen men, which accounted for half the killers.

A pattern of death was established for the others. One by one, it was said, bodies were found of men killed in a distinctive way: They were stabbed in the chest and their throats were cut, almost symbolically. The story was that "Billy" Rogers and his brother Lieuen traveled up the Rio Grande on King and Kenedy riverboats. They would attend fandangos and when certain individuals were pointed out, they would be coaxed outside, into the shadows, stabbed in the heart and their throats cut. True? No one knows for sure.

But on the lower Rio Grande a slashed throat was called Billy's mark. The general belief was that Billy Rogers got his revenge, murder for murder. Simple, direct acts of retribution were understood, and appreciated, on both sides of the border. Years later, Rogers told a friend that he and Lieuen accounted for all the cutthroat killers except a man known as Capt. Santos who fled deep into the interior of Mexico. Billy Rogers died on Dec. 17, 1877. He was 56, still a young man, but his health had been poor, complicated by an old throat wound. He is buried in Old Bayview Cemetery.

SOURCES

Barbour, Philip N. Journals of the Late Brevet Major. G. P. Putnam's Sons, New York, 1936.

Briscoe, Eugenia Reynolds. City by the Sea. Vantage Press, 1985.

Brooks, N. C. A Complete History of the Mexican War. Grigg, Elliot & Company, Philadelphia, 1851.

Corpus Christi Gazette. Jan. 1, Feb. 5, March 8, 1846.

Daily Picayune, New Orleans. July 19, 20, 22, 26, 28, Aug. 3, 10, 16, 19, 22, 27, 31, Sept. 8, 19, 1845.

Dana, Napoleon Jackson Tecumseh. Monterrey Is Ours! The Mexican War Letters of Lieutenant Dana, 1845-1847. Edited by Robert H. Ferrell. University of Kentucky Press, 1990.

De Voto, Bernard. The Year of Decision, 1846. Houghton, Mifflin, Boston, 1950.

Donnelly, George K. 1846 Letter. Bill Walraven Column, Oct. 10, 1985, Corpus Christi Caller.

Doubleday, Abner. My Life in the Old Army. Edited by Joseph Chance. TCU Press, 1998.

French, Samuel G. Two Wars: An Autobiography of Gen. Samuel G. French. Nashville, Tenn., 1901.

Frost, John. The Mexican War and Its Warriors. H. Mansfield Company, New Haven and Philadelphia, 1848.

Fry, J. Reese. A Life of Zachary Taylor. Grigg, Elliot, Philadelphia, 1848.

Furber, George C. The Twelve Months Volunteers. Cincinnati, 1850.

General Taylor and His Staff (no author). Grigg, Elliot, Philadelphia, 1848.

Grant, Ulysses S. Personal Memoirs of U. S. Grant, Volume 1. The Century Company, New York, 1903.

Henry, W. S. Campaign Sketches of the War with Mexico. Harper, New York, 1848.

Hitchcock, Ethan Allen. 1) Fifty Years in Camp and Field, edited by W. A. Croffut. G. P. Putnam & Sons, 1909. 2) Unpublished diary, Gilcrease Museum, Tulsa, copied for Friends of the Library, Corpus Christi.

Holman, Hamilton. Zachary Taylor, Soldier of the Republic. Bobbs-Merrill, Indianapolis, 1941.

Jarvis, N. S. An Army Surgeon's Notes of Frontier Service — Mexican War. Journal of the Military Service Institution of the United States, Vol. 41.

Johnson, Richard W. Memoir of General George H. Thomas. J.B. Lippincott & Company, Philadelphia, 1881.

Longstreet, James. From Manassas to Appomattox; Memoirs of the Civil War in America. J. B. Lippincott & Company, Philadelphia, 1896.

Masland, Charles. Unpublished letters by Sgt. Charles Masland, 3rd Infantry, Corpus Christi Central Library.

McCall, George A. Letters from the Frontiers. J. B. Lippincott & Company, 1868.

McClintock, William A. Journal of a Trip Through Texas and Northern Mexico, 1846-1847. Southwest Historical Quarterly, Vol. 34.

Meade, George Gordon. The Life and Letters of George Gordon Meade. Volume 1. Scribner's, New York, 1913.

Mundy, James and Shuttleworth, Earl G. Flight of the Grand Eagle, Charles G. Bryant. J. S. McCarthy Company, 1997.

Nichols, Edward J. Zach Taylor's Little Army. Doubleday, Garden City, New York, 1963.

Niles National Register, Baltimore, July 21, Aug. 9, Aug. 23, 1845; Jan. 2, 1846.

Noll, Arthur Howard. General Kirby Smith. The University Press, University of the South, Suwanee, Tenn., 1907.

Ohrt, Wallace. Defiant Peacemaker, Nicholas Trist in the Mexican War. Texas A&M Press, 1997.

Patch, Joseph Dorst. The Concentration of General Zachary Taylor's Army at Corpus Christi, Texas. Mission Printing, Corpus Christi, 1962,

Peck, John James. The Sign of the Eagle. Union-Tribune Publishing Company, 1970.

Porter, John B. A Medical History of General Zachary Taylor's Army of Occupation in Texas and Mexico. The Military Surgeon, Vol. 48.

Reeves, C. M. Adventures and Achievements of Americans, Henry Howe. George F. Tuttle, New York, 1858.

Seitz, Don Carlos. Braxton Bragg: General of the Confederacy. The State Company, 1924.

Smith, E. (Ephraim) Kirby. To Mexico With Scott; Letters of Captain E. Kirby Smith to His Wife. Harvard University Press, 1917.

Smith, E. (Edmund) Kirby. See Noll, Arthur Howard.

Smith, Isaac. Reminiscences of a Campaign in Mexico. Chapmans & Spann, Indianapolis, 1848.

Smith, Justin H. The War With Mexico. Macmillan Company, New York, 1919.

Thorpe, Thomas Bangs. Our Army on the Rio Grande. Carey and Hart, Philadelphia, 1846.

Turner, Josiah. Reminiscences of Early Days in Corpus Christi. Weekly Corpus Christi Caller, Jan. 24, 1908.

Whiting, Daniel Powers. A Soldier's Life. Nueces Press, Corpus Christi, 2011.

Wilcox, Cadmus M. History of the Mexican War. The Church News Publishing Company, Washington, D. C. 1892.

Wynne, James. Memoir of Major Samuel Ringgold. Read before the Maryland Historical Society and printed by John Murphy, Baltimore, 1847.

INDEX

213

Belden, Frederick (trader) 28, 30, 31, 179
Belden, Mauricia 30, 31, 80 (photo), 117, 179, 184
Belknap, William G. 56, 142, 193
Benjamin, Calvin 102, 193
Berry, Benjamin A. 46, 197
Berry, Henry W. 29, 57, 179
Bibb, John J. C. 195
Blake, Jacob E. 158-159, 179, 192to
Blalock, Archibald 196
Bliss, W. W. S. 5, 38, 56, 161, 179, 191
Bludworth, Capt. 16
Bombord, James V. 193
Booker, Jacob J. 193
Bourjett, Sarah (Great Western) 64, 131, 164, 179-180
Bowman, Andrew W. 195
Bradford, Edmund 192
Bragg, Braxton 8-9, 40, 87 (photo), 132, 145, 150, 153, 180, 189, 192, 199, 207
Brazos Santiago 17, 121, 125, 141
Brennan, Mrs. 206
Brice, Capt. 23
Britton, Forbes 151, 153, 176, 180, 194
Brooke, R. L. 194
Brooks, William T. H. 195
Brown, Jacob 90, 150, 152, 153, 164, 180, 183, 194, 203
Brown, Mr. and Mrs. 171
Bryant, Charles G. 104, 110, 117, 200, 207
Buchanan, James 4
Buchanan, Robert C. 195
Buell, Don Carlos 195
Buena Vista (battle of) 65, 168, 179, 180, 182, 184, 186, 187, 188
Burbank, John G. 193
Burke, Martin J. 193
Butcher, Joseph 196
Byars, Samuel 196
Byrne, Dr. Barnard M. 191

Callahan, Lawrence 196

---

* Capt. William Chapman of the 5th Infantry Regiment served as a colonel in the Union Army in the Civil War. He died in 1887 in Green Bay, Wisc. Capt. William W. Chapman, an army quartermaster, was stationed in Corpus Christi in the 1850s; he owned a sheep ranch on Santa Gertrudis Creek. He died at Fortress Monroe, Va., in 1859.

DeLeon, Dr. David C.   193
Denny, St. Clair (paymaster)   191
Dent, Julia   57
Denton, Jeremiah   196
Denton, Roswell   205
Desierto de los Muertos   133
De Voto, Bernard   2, 33, 205
Dimick, Justin   193
Dix, Roger S. (paymaster)   102, 191
Dobbins, Stephen D.   39, 59, 160
Donelson, Andrew J.   7
Donnelly, George K.   63, 205
Doubleday, Abner   37, 38, 105, 167, 182, 193, 205
Drane, Anthony   194
Druves, Jacob   196
Duncan, James   49, 123, 126, 156, 157-159, 188, 192
Dunn, Matthew   176

Eaton, Joseph   38, 161, 182, 191
Edgar, Jacob T.   196
Edwards, Richard   197
Eisenberger, John   196
Elzey, Arnold   193
Erving, John   53, 192
Eastman, Seth   74-75 (sketch of Corpus Christi)
Elliott, Edward G.   195
Engenspiehl, — —   196
E. S. Lamdin (ship)   32
Everitt, J. R.   28

Fahnestock, Simon S.   192
Falcon, Ramon   148, 182
Farelly, Patrick A.   195
Farry, Joseph F.   193
Fehrenbach, T. R.   54
Field, George P.   195
Filisola, Vicente   89. 133, 136
Fletcher, George W. (publisher)   108
Ford, John   196

Forrest, Elza B.   196
Forrey, William   196
Fort Brown (Fort Texas)   65, 90 (map), 144, 154, 164, 167, 180, 181, 183, 185-186, 190, 202, 203
Fort Jesup   1, 3, 4, 7-9, 38, 198, 199, 205
Fort Marcy   25, 33
Fort Paredes (Matamoros)   167
Fort Pike   43, 46
Foster, Capt.   126
Fowler, Daniel H.   196
Fowler, Sterne H.   194
Fowler, William   193
Foy, Patrick   196
Fraser, William   196
Fremont, Sewall L.   192
French, Samuel G.   25, 49, 57, 58, 102, 131, 134, 138, 182, 189, 192, 205
Furber, George   174-175, 206

Galloway, Robert   196
Gantt, Levi   145, 182, 194
Gardner, Franklin   194
Gardner, William   175
Garey, William   196
Garland, John   60, 101, 102, 132, 161, 195
Garnett, Robert S.   193
Gates, Collinson R.   193
Gates, William   9
Gatlin, Richard   145, 182, 194
Gazette, The Corpus Christi   65, 108-110, 125, 170, 171, 178, 181, 195, 200, 201, 205
Gettner, George   196
Gibson, Augustus A.   193
Gilham, William   193
Gill, Samuel   193
Gilpin, Henry A. (trader)   27
Glaevecke, Adolphus   206
Gleason, George   29
Goliad   102, 116, 139

Gonzales, F.   109
Goodhand, James   196
Gordon, William H.   195
Graham, Richard H.   47, 195
Graham, Capt. William M.   120-122, 195
Graham, Pvt. William   196
Grant, Ulysses S.   3, 4, 8, 21, 48, 49, 56, 57, 65, 81-82 (photos),
    102, 111, 118, 119, 127 - 129, 133, 137, 139, 141, 144, 148,
    154, 176, 179, 182, 183, 187, 188, 195, 200, 201, 206, 207
Grand Ecore   3, 8
Gray, Mabry (Mustang)   54, 172, 173, 183, 207
Guerra, Dom   206
Gussett, Norwick   176

Hamilton, Fowler   192
Hamilton, Holman   10, 33, 206
Handy, James O.   196
Hanson, Charles   194
Hardee, William J.   120-122, 149, 165, 183, 192, 203
Hart, Mrs. (actress)   111
Hatch, David   172
Hatch, John P.   195
Hatheway, John S.   193
Hawkins, Edgar S.   153, 154, 183, 194
Hawkins, Dr. Hamilton S. (and Mrs. Hawkins)   55, 183, 192
Hayman, Samuel B.   194
Hayne, Rev. John   116
Hays, Alexander   161, 183
Hays, John C.   54, 183-184
Hays, William   192
Hazlitt, Robert   195
Hearty, Ardel   196
Hellan, Francis   196
Helmuller, F. (merchant)   109
Henderson, Gov. J. Pinckney   117, 171, 185
Henerman, Henry   196
Henry, Thomas M.   194
Henry, William S.   10, 11, 14, 15, 25, 30, 31, 39, 40, 41, 47, 49,

53, 58, 59, 62, 98, 103, 106, 110, 115, 118, 122, 127, 129, 130, 137, 139, 141, 142, 143, 145, 146, 148, 165, 184, 195, 206

Lawrence (brig)   126
Lee, Arthur T.   193
Lee, Francis   194
Lewars, John   197
Lincoln, George   193
Linn, John J. (trader)   27
Live Oak Point   17, 27
Longstreet, James   86 (photo), 104, 110, 154, 158, 159, 179,
   186, 193, 206
Los Pintos Creek   130
Love, James   54
Lovell, Mansfield   192
Low, John   16
Lowd, Allen   150, 151, 152, 185, 193
Lowry, Albert   192
Lugenbuhl, John   197
Lugenbeel, Pinkney   194
Luther, Roland A.   193
Lydia Ann Channel   16

Maclay, Robert P.   193
McCall, Edward   197
McCall, George A.   60, 99, 107, 119, 128, 132, 160, 162, 185,
   195, 207
McClelland, George C.   195
McClintock, William (traveler)   173-174, 207
McCown, John P.   193
McFerran, John C.   195
McGloin's Bluff   17, 46
McIntosh, James S.   53, 56, 126, 159, 185, 194
McKavett, Henry   193
McKerns, Daniel   197
McLowlen, John   197
McLaws, Lafayette   103, 185-186
McPhail, Dr. Leonard C.   192
McRee, Samuel   191

Magruder, John B.   104, 110, 186, 193
Mainlan, James   16

---

* Capt. Moses Merrill of the 5th Infantry was killed Sept. 8, 1847 at Molino del Rey. Fort Merrill on the Nueces River was named in his honor.

Pemberton, John C.   192
Pettigrew, Ellen   117
Picayune (ship)   24
Pitcher, Thomas G.   194
Point Isabel (Frontone)   126, 141-142, 146, 150, 154, 159, 163,
   202, 203
Point Isabel Road   156
Polk, President James K.   1, 3, 18, 51, 59, 165
Porpoise (Navy brig)   126
Porter, Giles   193
Porter, Dr. John B.   68, 194, 208
Porter, Theodoric   111, 148, 187, 195
Port Lavaca   113, 175
Potter, Joseph H.   194
Puebla (battle of)   168
Pugh, John M.   197

Queen Victoria (ship)   10, 11
Quinn, Pat   172

Rains, Gabriel J.   194
Ramirez. Patricio   206
Ramsay, George D.   192
Ransom, Owen P.   64, 187
Redmond, Henry (trader)   28
Reeve, Isaac V.D.   69, 187, 193
Reeves, C. M.   40, 101, 118, 134, 208
Reifstack, Andrew   197
Resaca de la Palma (battle of)   51, 92 (art), 94 (map), 159,
   165-171, 175, 178-189, 203-204
Reynolds, Eugenia   205
Reynolds, John F.   86 (photo), 99, 109, 182, 187, 189, 192
Reynolds, Joseph J.   193
Richardson, Israel B.   195
Richardson, John F. B.   197
Richey, John   161, 188, 195
Riddle, James   197
Ridgely, Randolph   58, 111-113, 130, 157, 160, 161, 188, 192
Ringgold, Samuel   26, 49, 91 (art), 123, 124, 156, 157-159, 182,

188, 192, 209

Rio Grande   4, 5, 7, 18, 28, 35, 39, 51, 65, 89, 90, 97, 110, 115, 116-120, 121-129, 131, 133, 139, 140-144, 159, 162, 167, 172, 173, 176, 178, 181, 184, 201, 202, 204, 208

Roberts, William   16

Robinson, John C.   194

Rogers, Anderson   205

Rogers, Elizabeth   205

Rogers, Lieuen   207

Rogers, Patterson   205 - 207

Rogers, William L. "Billy"   205 - 207

Roland, John F.   192

Root, W.   194

Rosecrants, Mortimer   194

Ross, Richard H.   194

Rossell, Nathan Beaks   194

Ruggles, Daniel   194

Russell, James W.   194

Sackett, Delos B.   192

St. Joseph's Island   11, 13, 14-18, 24, 31, 32, 42, 46, 47, 49, 54, 112, 114, 125, 172, 174, 175, 180, 191, 192, 198, 199

St. Mary's (Navy ship)   11

Saltillo   65, 148, 168, 176, 182

San Antonio   7, 26, 40, 41, 102, 103, 172, 185, 190, 200

Sandoval, Chipito   45, 147, 199

Sanders, John   191

Sanders, Michael   197

Sands, The   133-137

San Patricio   26, 27, 29, 38, 40, 41, 51, 56, 103, 199

Santa Gertrudis   122, 131, 170, 201

Sarah Foyle (ship)   32

Saunders, William H.   192

Scarritt, Jeremiah   56, 188, 191

Scott, John B.   193

Scott, John B.   194

Scott, Martin   60, 194

Scott, Winfield   31, 104, 105, 168, 176, 184

Screven, Richard B.   193

---

* Brothers Ephraim Kirby Smith and Edmund Kirby Smith used the name E. Kirby Smith. Both were at Corpus Christi with Taylor's army. Ephraim was killed in the battle of Molino del Rey. Edmund became a Confederate general in the Civil War.

Taylor, Gen. Zachary   4-5, ordered to Texas; 7-9, departure from Fort Jesup; 10-11, boarded steamship bound for Texas coast; 16-18, decided on Corpus Christi as location to concentrate the army; 19-21, encountered difficulties in crossing shallow mudflats; 21-22, eschews uniform, fancy dress; 31 dined at Mauricia Belden's home; issued first order from Corpus Christi; 33, criticized for not following military sanitation rules; 38-40, rode with aides to meet dragoons, who marched overland to Texas; 68, decided tents would suffice for winter quarters; 77-78, illustrations; 101, drummer boy cut tent cords; 105, brevet quarrel roils camp; 107, celebrates New Year's Day; 115, ordered to Rio Grande; 117, general danced at Annexation Ball; 120-121, sent reconnaissance patrols to scout route for march; 125, issued marching orders; 136-137, expected opposition in crossing Arroyo Colorado; 142, flag hoisted on Rio Grande and work started on building fortifications; 150, marched to Point Isabel, base of supplies; 154-165, first battles of war fought on Texas' side of the river; 167, crossed the river and occupied Matamoros; 168, took Camargo, Monterrey; 188-189, elected president and death in office.
Thomas, C.   191
Thomas, George H.   83 (photo), 189, 192, 206
Thompson, James L.   194
Thorpe, T. B.   143, 208
Thornton, Seth B.   149, 150, 189, 192, 203
Three Mile Point   30
Tijerina, Miguel   206
Turner, Josiah   62, 189, 208
Twelve-Mile Motts   128-129
Twiggs, David E.   9, 38, 40, 41, 53, 56, 57, 64, 65, 84 (photo), 104, 105, 106, 110, 126, 144, 146, 159, 167, 176, 189, 192, 204
Tyler, President John   1

Undine (lighter)   13, 18, 19, 22-24, 32
Union Theater   103-104, 110, 116, 117, 186, 200, 201

Valere, —— (Grant's hired servant)   56
Van Allmen, Gutlich   197

Van Bokkelen, William K.   194
Van Dorn, Earl   164, 190, 194
Van Horne, Jefferson   195
Vega, Romula Diaz de la   160
Veracruz   168
Victoria (schooner)   110
Vose, Josiah   8, 53

Wade, William W.   197
Waggaman, George G.   191
Wainwright, George   194
Walker, Andy   172
Wallen, Henry D.   195
Walnut Springs   175
Warner, Ulysses W.   197
Weld, Thomas B. J.   193
Wells, James B.   16
Wells, Dr. John B.   192
West, —— —   197
Whipple, Joseph H.   194
Whistler, William   53, 56, 106, 123, 126, 129, 190, 194
Whitall, John A.   194
White Wing (ship)   32
Whiting, Daniel P.   42, 43, 55, 64, 65, 70-71 (drawing of
    encampment), 79 (photo), 128, 131, 140, 142, 147, 148, 151,
    153, 163, 164, 169, 181, 190, 194, 209
Whiting, Henry M.   193, 194
Whiting, Indiana   148
Wilcox, Cadmus M.   175, 209
William Ivy (ship)   42
Williams, Seth   193
Williamson, Andrew J.   195
Wilson, Joseph   197
Winship, Oscar F.   192
Woessner, Mollie   117
Wolf, D. (merchant)   109
Woodbury (ship)   126
Wood, Dr. Robert C.   194
Wood, William H.   194

FROM NUECES PRESS

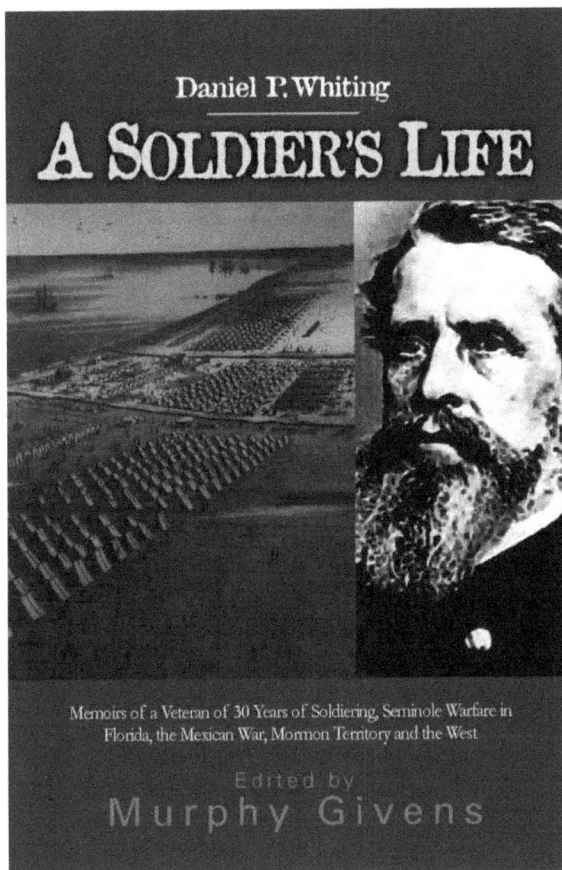

Memoirs of a Veteran of 30 Years of Soldiering, Seminole
Warfare in Florida, the Mexican War, Mormon Territory
and the West

www.nuecespress.com

MORE BOOKS AVAILABLE FROM NUECES PRESS

1919 – The Storm
Corpus Christi – A History
A Soldier's Life
Great Tales from the History of South Texas
Recollections of Other Days
Perilous Trails of Texas
Columns   2009 – 2011
Columns 2 2012 – 2013
Columns 3 2014 – 2015
Columns 4 2016 – 2018
Streets of Corpus Christi Texas
Thomas Noakes - Diary of War & Drought
100 Tales of Old Texas
Water Woes

Copies are available from

www.nuecespress.com